W9-BGE-578

MIND'S EYE

THUNDER BAY
P·R·E·S·S

San Diego, California

Thunder Bay Press

An imprint of the Advantage Publishers Group

5880 Oberlin Drive, San Diego, CA 92121-4794

www.thunderbaybooks.com

ISBN-13: 978-1-59223-574-2
ISBN-10: 1-59223-574-3

Printed and bound in China
1 2 3 4 5 10 09 08 07 06

Mind's Eye is a brand-new collection of user-friendly puzzles designed especially to stimulate the visual imagination of those who love twisting, turning, and probing a problem in their mind until they arrive at the right answer. Some solutions will come right away, while it may take a little more time and concentration to find the right path with other puzzles. But however you go about tackling a problem, there is (usually!) only one answer.

We each hold a different idea of the world in our own mind's eye, and this can also be very different from culture to culture as well as from person to person. Getting from A to B is a very simple case in point. If you were to ask several friends to tell you the route to the nearest store or café, you would find that the replies vary greatly. One person might concentrate solely on local landmarks or other well-known locations, whereas someone else might see the route in terms of other routes they know and so describe friends' houses or places that are personal to their own experiences. Such experiments have been tried with children who were asked to draw a map of their local neighborhood. Each child's map was very different and accentuated aspects of the landscape in a multitude of ways. This is because everyone perceives the world in their own unique fashion. Different people depend on different visual "signposts" to help them understand their environment.

It is this understanding that we modify continuously as we discover more and more about the world through our own experiences. Our brains have the job of making sense of the images that we see, but sometimes they give incorrect information. This can have positive results, however, as when we view an optical illusion or even visit the cinema.

Watching a movie is a classic example of how our tools of perception are fooled into thinking we see real movement on the screen. In actual fact, the action we witness is made up of a series of still images flashed before our eyes, so fast that we believe what our eyes show us. Real life works in the same way. When we blink, we miss the tiniest pieces of visual information. The brain fills in these minute gaps with an assumed perception. Our lives are more like the movies than we ever thought possible!

We can assure you that this book does nothing to fool your senses but instead should inspire you to give the world a closer look. If you're tackling the puzzles with your friends or family, you might find that each person goes about solving the puzzles in very different ways. In the end, all methods are valid, unless of course you get the wrong answer! But we learn something even when we make mistakes.

By the time you've completed this book, you'll be a master of observation, having boosted your powers of perception and stimulated that all-important puzzle-solving tool—your mind's eye. ✪

—David Popey

1 DIFFICULTY ⭐☆⭐☆⭐☆☆⭐☆  **Minutes**

Follow the arrows in the grid below to get to the yellow star.

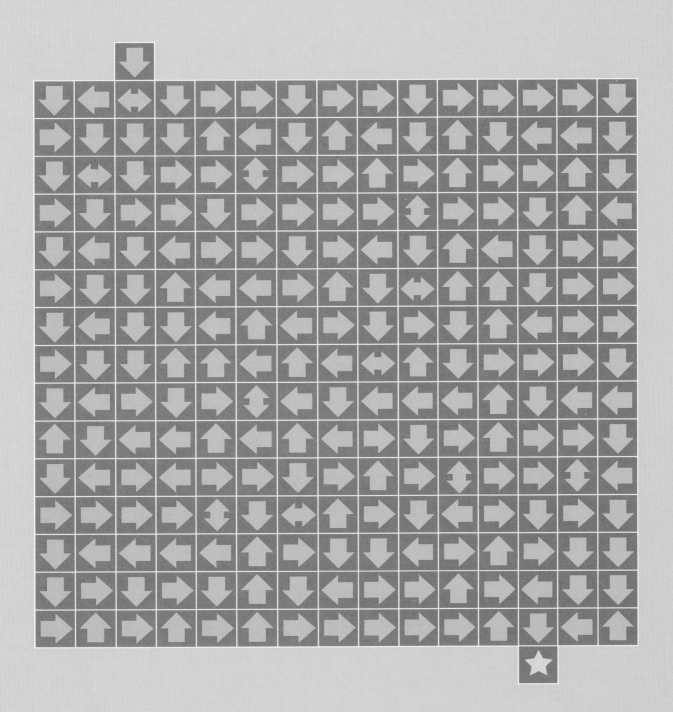

2 DIFFICULTY ✪✪✪✪✪✪✪✪✪  **5** Minutes

Which of the figures below (a, b, or c) completes the grid?

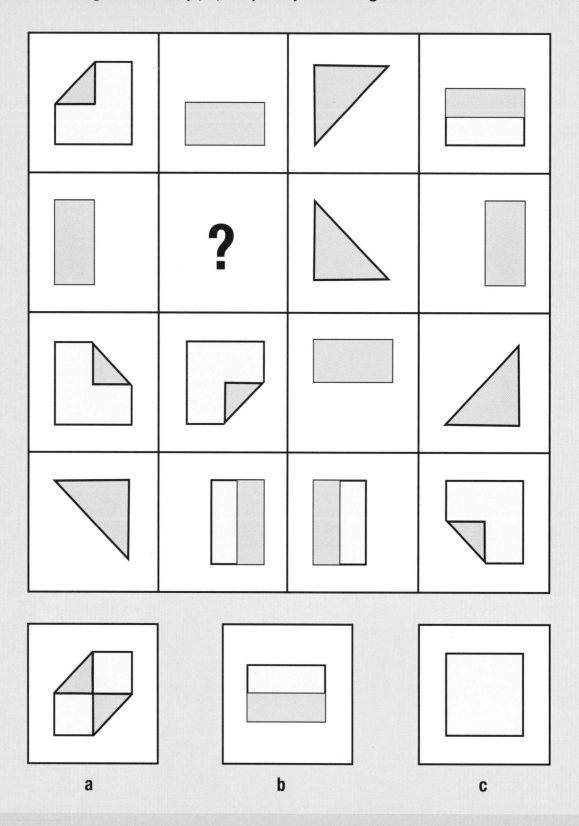

a   b   c

3 DIFFICULTY

Study this picture for two minutes, then see if you can answer the questions on page 10.

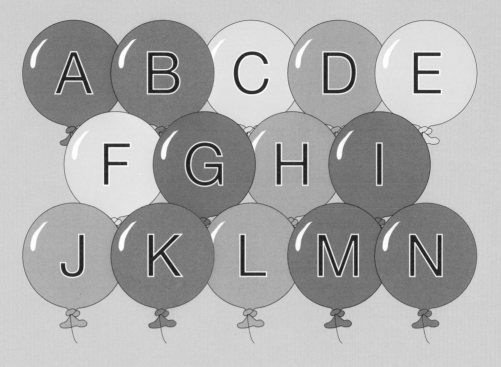

4 DIFFICULTY

Here are ten matches. How can you take one away but still be left with ten?

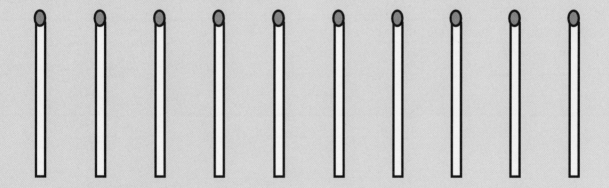

[3] DIFFICULTY ✪✪✪✪✪✪✪✪✪✪

 3 Minutes

Can you answer these questions about the puzzle on page 9 without looking back?

1. Which letter appears on the green balloon?

2. How many balloons are orange?

3. What is the color of balloon G?

4. What letter appears on the balloon touching both balloon L and balloon M?

5. What is the color of balloon B?

6. What is the color of the balloon below and to the left of balloon F?

7. Which balloon color appears most often in the picture?

8. How many balloons are in the picture?

5 DIFFICULTY ✪✪✪✪✪✪✪✪✪✪

 5 Minutes

Using four straight lines only, can you divide this tree into six sections, each containing the leaves of five different trees?

6 **DIFFICULTY** ✪✪✪✪✪✪✩✩✩✩  **8** Minutes

In each of the four buildings below, one type of brick is used less frequently than it is in the other three buildings. Can you discover the different brick in each construction? The ten brick types are as follows:

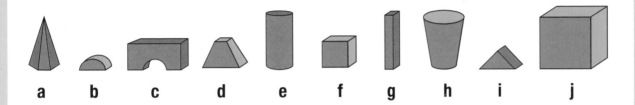

a   b   c   d   e   f   g   h   i   j

Building 1

Building 2

Building 3

Building 4

7 DIFFICULTY ✪✪✪✪✩✩✩✩✩✩  **3** Minutes

Which of the four boxed figures (a, b, c, or d) completes the set?

8 DIFFICULTY ✪✪✪✪✪✩✩✩✩✩

(2) Minutes

Rosemary's magic mirror reflects very strangely! Can you match each duck to its correct (although misplaced and somewhat distorted) image in the mirror?

9 DIFFICULTY ★★★☆☆☆☆☆☆☆ **5** Minutes

Given that scales a and b balance perfectly, how many triangles are needed to balance scale c?

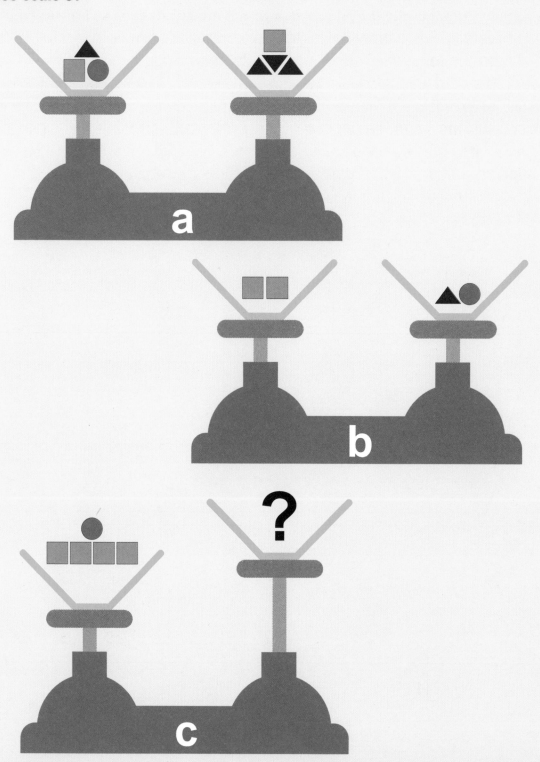

10 DIFFICULTY ✪✪✪✪✪✪✩✩✩✩

 **Minutes**

Kirsty played a game of Snakes and Ladders with her brother Tom. He threw the first 6, so started first, placing his playing piece on the 6. After that, every time it was Kirsty's turn, her die followed the sequence 4, 2, 6, 3, 5, 1; so her first move was to square 4, then square 6, etc. After his first turn when he threw the 6, Tom's die followed the sequence 1, 5, 4, 3, 2, 6 each time, so his second move was to square 7, his third was to square 12, etc. The normal rules of the game were followed, so whenever someone landed on a square that had the foot of a ladder, the piece was moved to the top of the ladder. Whenever someone landed on a square that had the head of a snake, the piece was moved to the tail of the snake. The number thrown to end the game didn't necessarily matter, since the first person to move a piece completely off the board won. Who won the game—Kirsty or Tom?

100	99	98	97	96	95	94	93	92	91
81	82	83	84	85	86	87	88	89	90
80	79	78	77	76	75	74	73	72	71
61	62	63	64	65	66	67	68	69	70
60	59	58	57	56	55	54	53	52	51
41	42	43	44	45	46	47	48	49	50
40	39	38	37	36	35	34	33	32	31
21	22	23	24	25	26	27	28	29	30
20	19	18	17	16	15	14	13	12	11
1	2	3	4	5	6	7	8	9	10

START →

11 DIFFICULTY ✪✪✪✪✪✩✩✩✩✩  3 Minutes

By touching one coin only, make two rows of three heads. You may not turn any coins over.

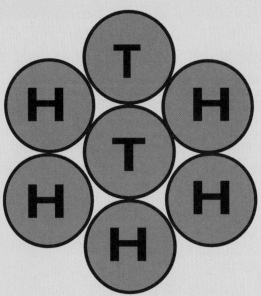

12 DIFFICULTY ✪✪✪✪✪✩✩✩✩✩  3 Minutes

Which three differently colored pieces can be fitted together to form a copy of this star? Pieces may be rotated, but not flipped over.

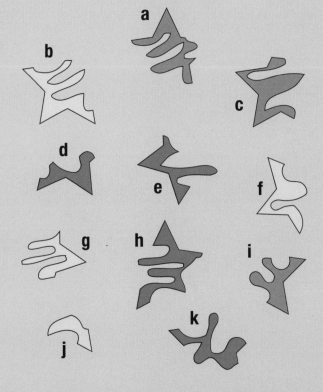

13 DIFFICULTY ✪✪✪✪✪✪✫✫✫✫  **Minutes**

Place the cards on the left into the colored grid so that each horizontal row and vertical column contains an ace, two, three, four, and five of hearts; and each shape (shown by the different colors) also contains an ace, two, three, four, and five of hearts. Some cards are already in their correct positions.

14 DIFFICULTY ✪✪✪✪✪✪✫✫✫✫ **4** **Minutes**

By drawing three straight lines, can you divide this circle into five sections, each containing two green stars, one red star, one yellow star, one blue star, and one black star?

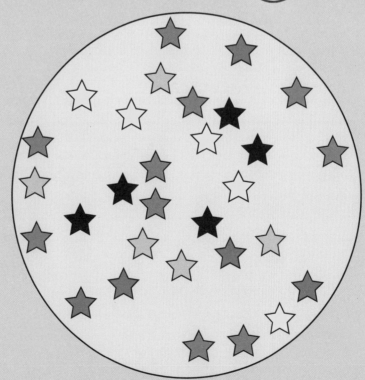

15 DIFFICULTY ★★☆☆☆☆☆☆☆☆

4 Minutes

Our rower is looking for an island on which to rest. Unfortunately, each island is inhabited by a small devil, though one is more hospitable than the others. Can you figure out which island he reaches by following the directions below?

1R, 3D, 1L, 5D, 2R, 3U, 1L, 2D, 4R, 1D, 1L, 4U, 1R, 1D, 2L, 3U, 3L, 1U, 2R, 1U, 1R, 1D, 1R, 1U, 1R, 3D, 3L, 1D, 1L

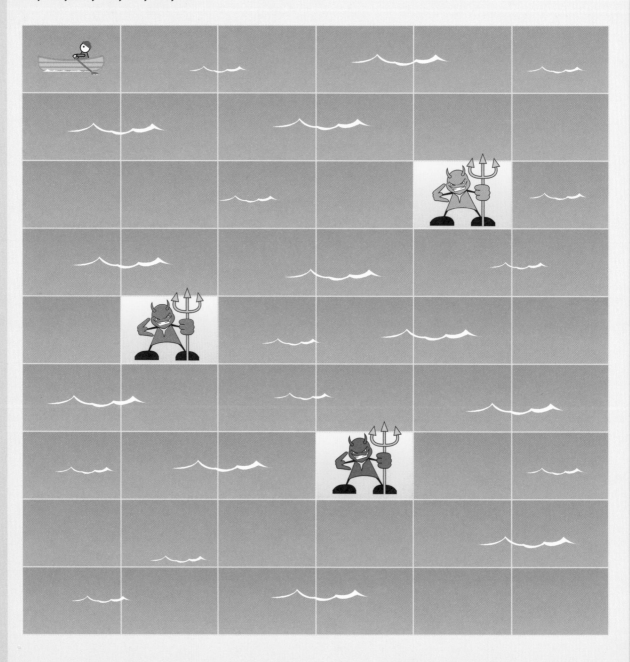

16 DIFFICULTY ✪✪✪✪✪✪✪✪✪✪  4 Minutes

This grid of dominoes should have the same total of spots in each row and column, but two pieces have been moved out of position. Can you put them back in the right place?

17 DIFFICULTY ✪✪✪✪✪✪✪✪✪✪ 4 Minutes

Can you pair up these door keys with the imprints of their ends?

a

b

c

d

e

f

1

6

2

3

4

5

18 DIFFICULTY ✪✪✪✪✪✪✪✪✪✪

30 Minutes

Don't let this numbergram put you out to pasture.

HOW TO DO A NUMBERGRAM:

Along each row or column, there are numbers that indicate how many blocks of black squares are in a line. For example, "3, 4, 5" indicates that from left to right or top to bottom, there is a group of three black squares, then a group of four black squares, then another group of five black squares.

Each block of black squares on the same line must have at least one white square between it and the next block of black squares. Blocks of black squares may or may not have a number of white squares before and after them.

It is sometimes possible to determine which squares will be black without reference to other lines or columns. It is helpful to put a small dot in a square you know will be empty.

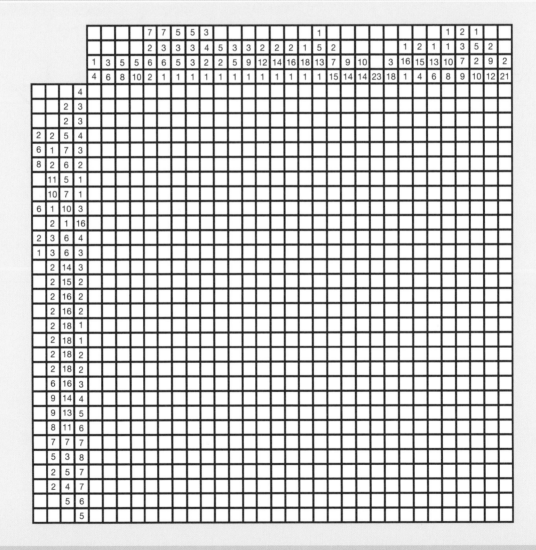

Using three straight lines, can you divide this star into six sections, each containing six different shapes?

20 DIFFICULTY ✪✪✪✪✪✪✩✩✩✩  5 Minutes

Using yellow, red, blue, and green only, can you color this map so that no two touching areas have the same color?

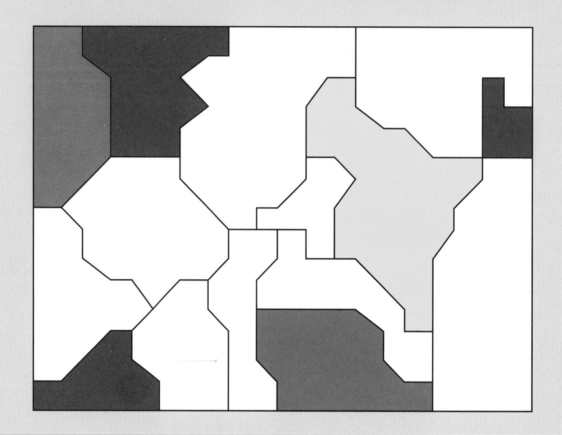

21 DIFFICULTY ✪✪✪✪✪✪✩✩✩✩ 4 Minutes

What should the hour hand point to on clock d in this sequence?

a   b   c   d

22 DIFFICULTY ✪✪✪✪✪✪✰✰✰✰  **5** Minutes

Which of the four squares (a, b, c, or d) should go in the center of the grid?

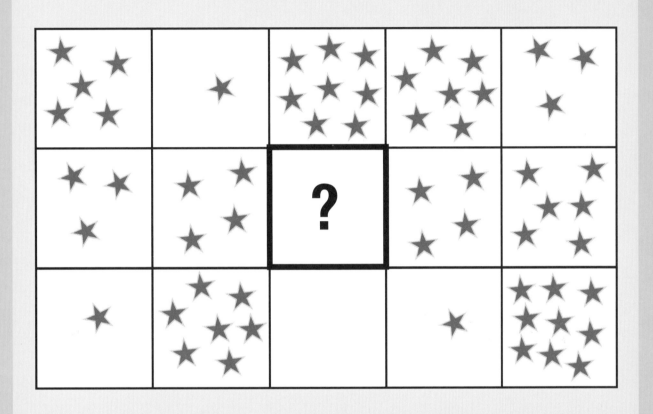

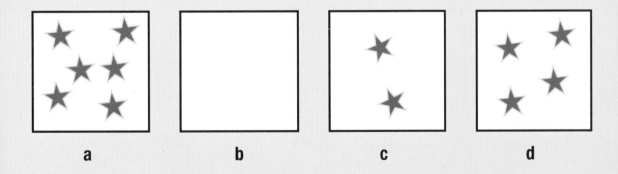

a   b   c   d

23 DIFFICULTY  Minutes

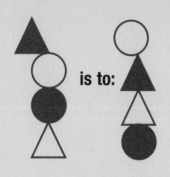 is to: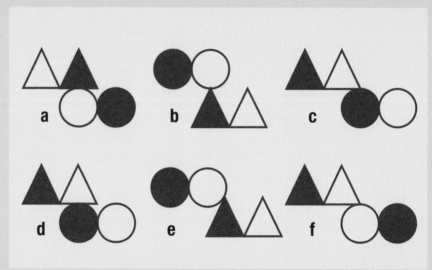

as  is to:

24 DIFFICULTY  Minutes

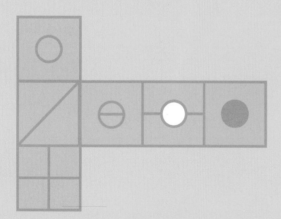

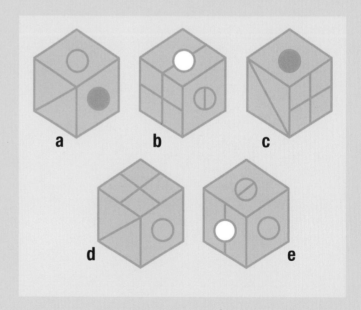

When the above is folded to form a cube, which one of the options opposite (a, b, c, d, or e) is produced?

25 DIFFICULTY ✪✪✪✪✪✪☆☆☆☆  5 Minutes

Which of the four boxed figures (a, b, c, or d) completes the set?

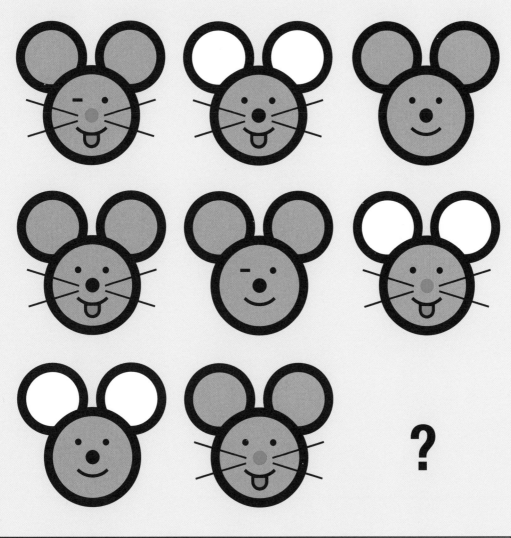

?

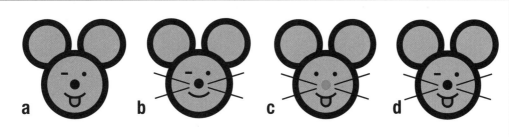

a b c d

In the game of solitaire, the aim is to jump one blue disk over another (horizontally or vertically), removing the disk you jumped over from the board until only one piece remains. Jumps can occur only over one disk, and you must land on an empty space. The aim is to end up with just one blue disk remaining.

On this unusual board, a few of the squares have been left blank. You must remain within the area marked out by the game board at all times. There may be more than one solution. You could use a piece of squared paper and some coins to play this game.

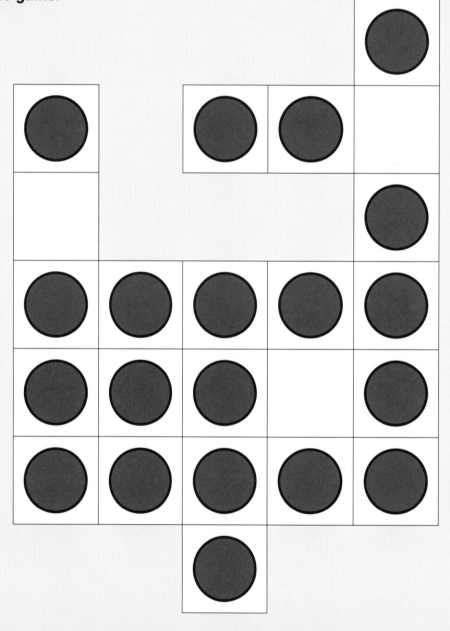

27 DIFFICULTY ✪✪✪✪✫✫✫✫✫✫  **Minutes**

At 4:00 p.m. on February 26, 2000, Jason started his course work. He expected it to take him 86 minutes, but he finished a quarter-hour early. So he left immediately for a vacation and returned exactly a week later. What time and date was it on Jason's digital 24-hour watch when he returned?

28 DIFFICULTY ✪✫✫✫✫✫✫✫✫✫  **Minutes**

By drawing three straight lines, can you divide this polygon into five sections, each containing seven different shapes?

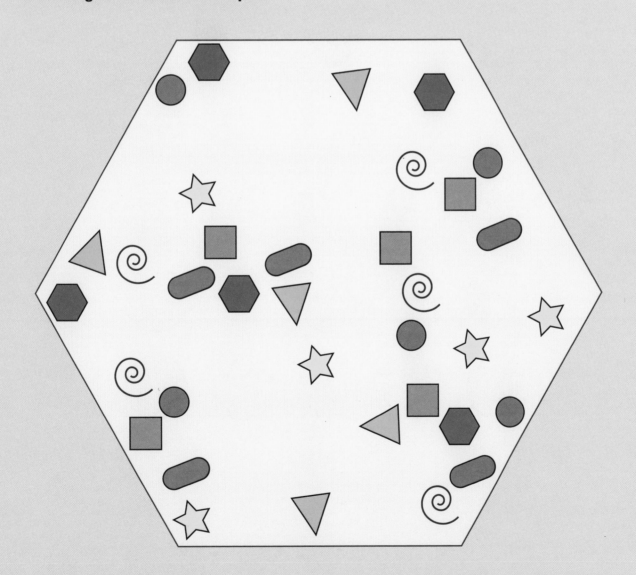

29 DIFFICULTY ✪✪✪✪✪✪✪☆☆ ⏱ **5** Minutes

There are two identical pairs among these nine bottles. Can you spot them?

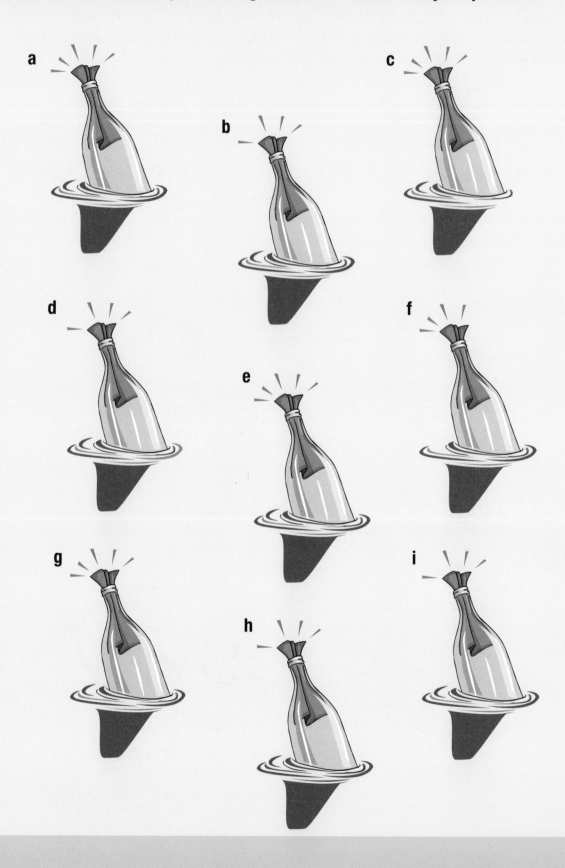

30 DIFFICULTY ✪✩✩✪✩✪✩✩✩✩ **6** Minutes

Only two of these patterns are the same. Can you spot the identical pair?

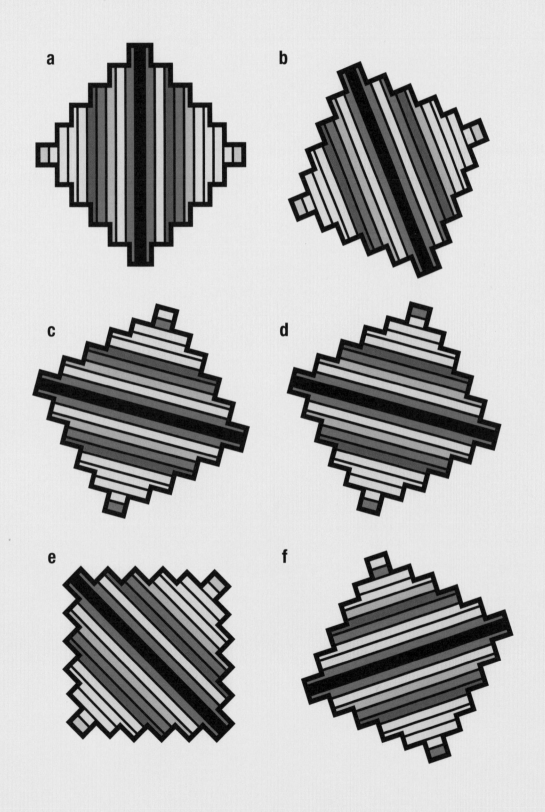

a

b

c

d

e

f

31 DIFFICULTY ✪✪✪✪✪✪☆☆☆☆ **5** Minutes

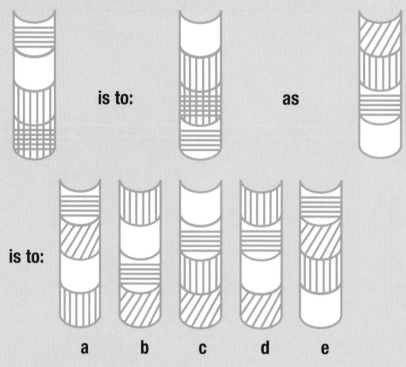

is to:

a b c d e

32 DIFFICULTY ✪✪✪✪✪✪☆☆☆☆ **4** Minutes

Which two of these squares are the same shade as the one at the bottom right?

33 DIFFICULTY ✪✪✪✪✪✪✪☆☆  **6** Minutes

Can you fit the two sets of colored shapes into the shaded areas in this tangram puzzle? Pieces may be rotated, but not flipped over, and no piece may overlap another. (Hint: each figure is made up of one set of pieces.)

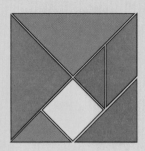

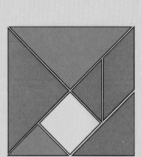

34 DIFFICULTY ✪✪✪✪✪✪☆☆☆  **4** Minutes

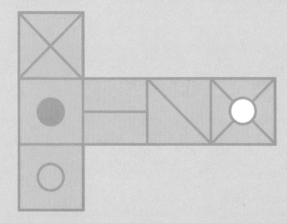

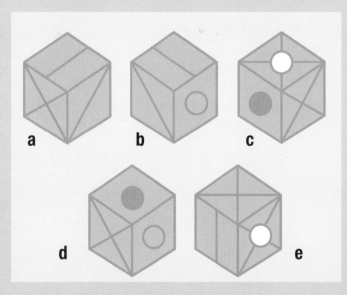

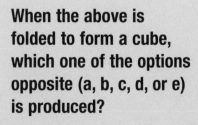

When the above is folded to form a cube, which one of the options opposite (a, b, c, d, or e) is produced?

35 DIFFICULTY ✪✪✪✪✪✩✩✩✩  **4** Minutes

Which of the four boxed figures (a, b, c, or d) completes the set?

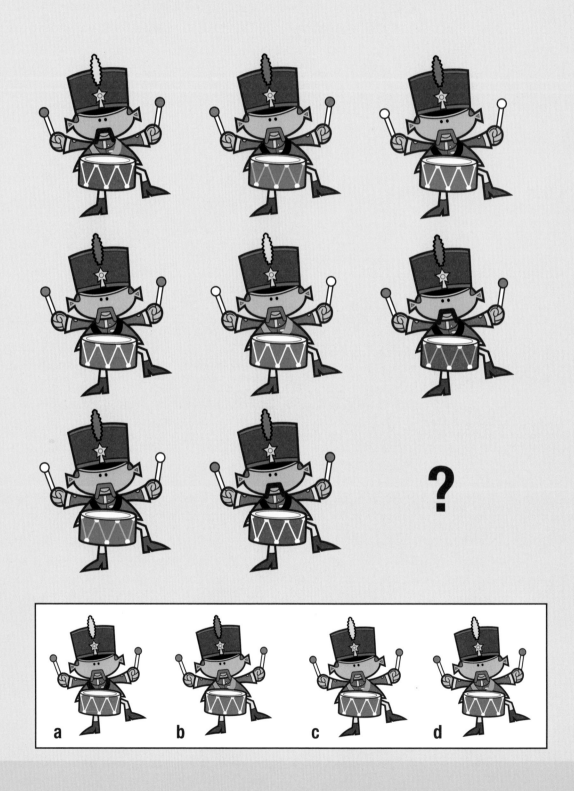

36 DIFFICULTY ⭐⭐⭐⭐⭐☆☆☆☆☆  4 Minutes

Which of the four boxed structures (a, b, c, or d) completes the set?

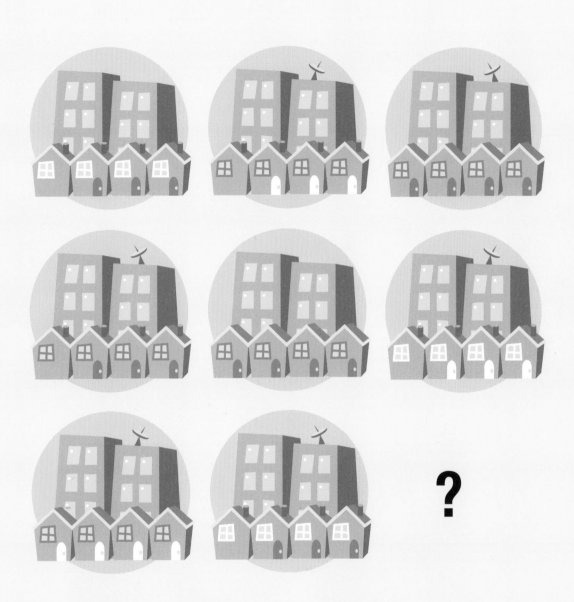

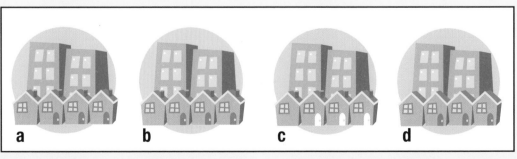

37 DIFFICULTY ✪✪✪✪✪☆☆☆☆☆ ⑤ Minutes

Two mathematics professors meet regularly for a game of dominoes. When Professor Gauss asked his friend how many years he had been playing the game, Professor Euler replied by laying out these dominoes in a row. What was the answer?

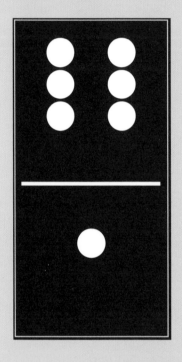
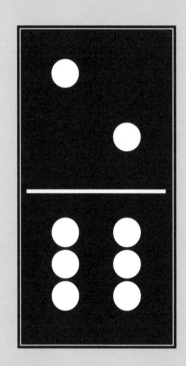
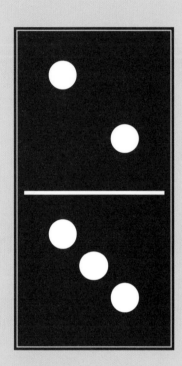
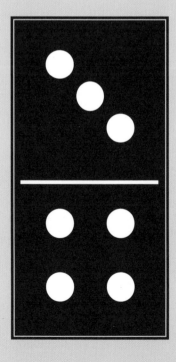
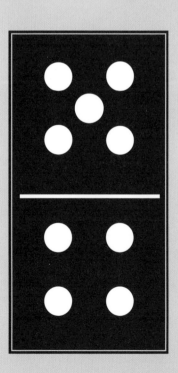

38 DIFFICULTY ⚝⚝⚝✩✩✩✩✩✩✩

8 Minutes

Jane tidied her shelves the other day, then realized that she had misplaced some of the objects. Can you spot how many items from the top picture are now missing in the lower picture? Circle them in the top drawing.

39 DIFFICULTY ✪✪✪✪✪✪☆☆☆☆  **Minutes**

Which of the figures below (a, b, c, d, e, or f) is the odd one out?

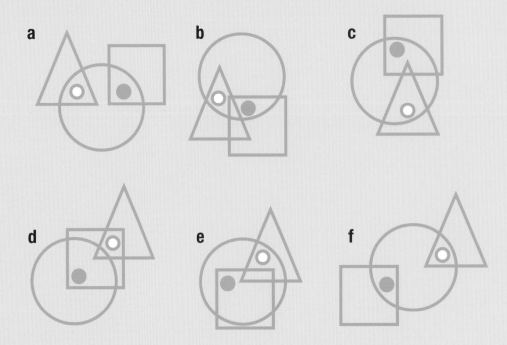

40 DIFFICULTY ✪✪✪✪✪☆☆☆☆☆  **Minutes**

Can you fit the colored shapes below into the shaded area in this tangram puzzle? Pieces may be rotated, but not flipped over, and no piece may overlap another.

41 DIFFICULTY ⊛⊛⊛⊛⊛⊛✩✩✩✩  **5** Minutes

Can you color this map using yellow, red, blue, and green only so that no two touching areas are the same? This rule doesn't apply to areas that touch at a corner point only.

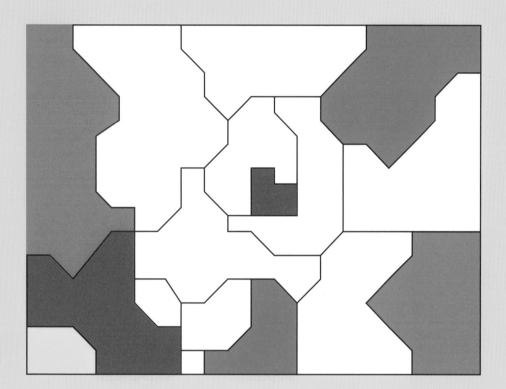

42 DIFFICULTY ⊛⊛⊛⊛⊛⊛✩✩✩✩ **4** Minutes

What should the minute hand point to on clock d in this sequence?

a   b   c   d

43 DIFFICULTY ✪✪✪✪✪✪✪✪✪✪

 30 Minutes

You'll be barking by the time you finish this numbergram. Make the connections between the numbers to complete the picture. See page 20 for advice on how to complete this kind of puzzle.

Column clues (top):

		3	6											12					
2	2	5	2	2	10	8	6	5	7	6		3	5		1	14		15	
5	1	1	3	3	5	1	3	3	2	1	3	3	1	4	12	3	1	14	1	16	17		19
2	4	6	1	1	2	2	2	2	2	7	6	6	7	6	6	10	8	7	6	2	2	2	2	1	1	18	1	20	20	20

Row clues (left):

		2	1
		3	2
		4	3
		4	4
	5	1	3
		7	4
		5	6
		5	8
		5	9
	2	1	11
	2	1	12
	2	1	13
		2	13
		1	14
	1	2	13
1	2	2	12
2	4	2	11
2	3	2	10
	2	3	11
2	1	6	9
	3	13	8
		20	7
	4	15	8
	2	12	6
	2	10	5
	9	2	6
	5	2	4
		2	3
		2	4
		2	1

44 DIFFICULTY ✪✪✪✪✪✪✩✩✩  3 Minutes

Which of the three squares below (a, b, or c) should go in the center of the grid?

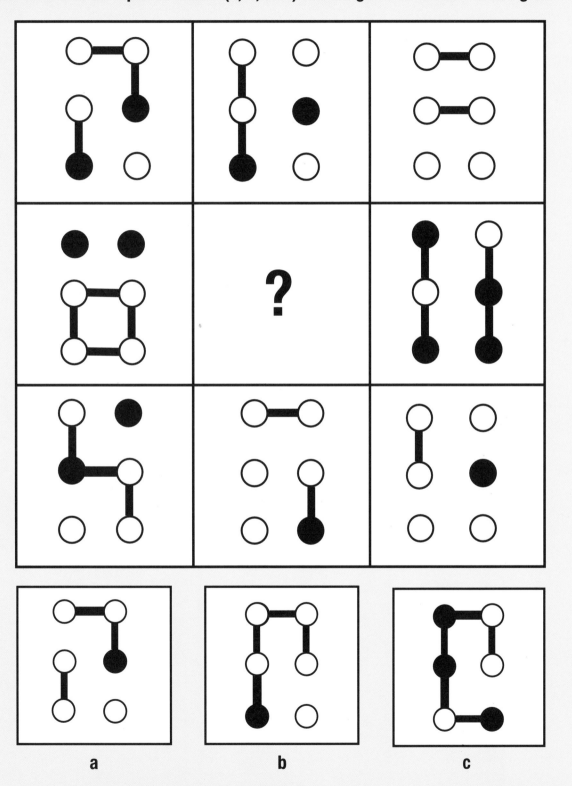

a   b   c

45 DIFFICULTY ✪✪✪✪✪✪☆☆☆☆☆ **5** Minutes

When the shape below is folded to form a cube, which one of the following (a, b, c, d, or e) can be produced?

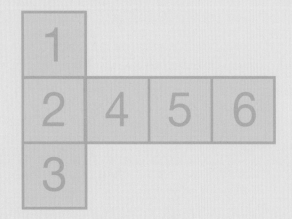

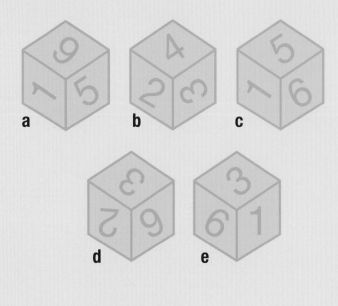

46 DIFFICULTY ✪✪✪✪✪☆☆☆☆☆☆ **2** Minutes

Use five matches to make five identical triangles.

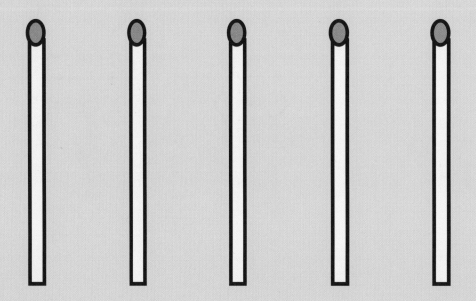

47 DIFFICULTY  Minutes

Can you fit the colored shapes below into the shaded area in this tangram puzzle? Pieces may be rotated, but not flipped over, and no piece may overlap another.

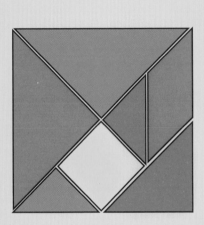

48 DIFFICULTY  Minutes

Again, can you fit the colored shapes below into the shaded area in this tangram puzzle? Pieces may be rotated, but not flipped over, and no piece may overlap another.

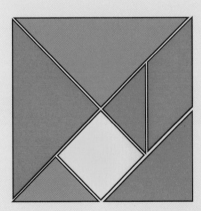

49 **DIFFICULTY** ✪✪✪✪✪✩✪✩✩  **Minutes**

Can you get from the diving board to the center of the pool through the circular maze?

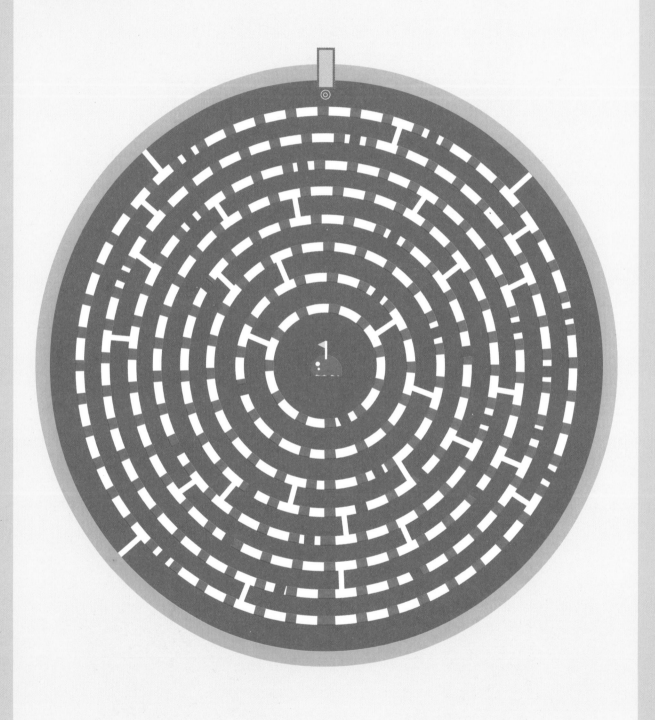

50 DIFFICULTY ⭐⭐⭐⭐⭐⭐☆☆☆☆

 **Minutes**

Only two of these fish are identical. Can you tell which?

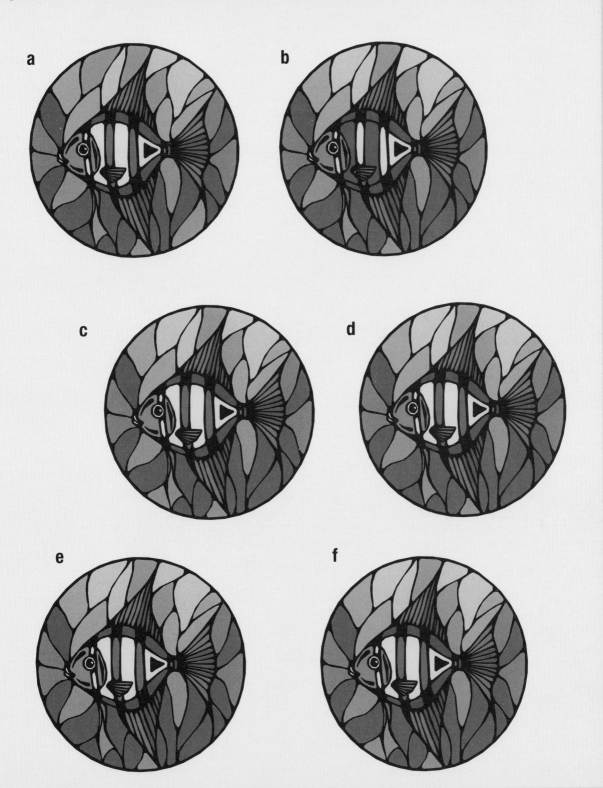

51 DIFFICULTY ✪✪✪✪✪✪✩✩✩✩

 **3** Minutes

Using three straight lines only, can you divide this field into five sections, each containing two of every type of animal? Within each section, no two animals of the same type should be looking in the same direction.

52 DIFFICULTY ✪✪✪✪✪✩✩✩✩✩

5 Minutes

Which four pieces can fit together to match the beach ball below? Any piece may be rotated, but not flipped over.

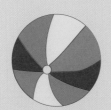

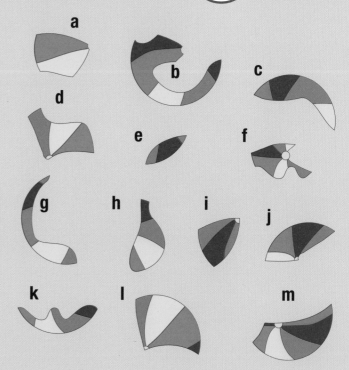

53 DIFFICULTY ✪✪✪✪✪✪✪✪✪✪ 5 Minutes

 is to:  as

is to:

     a   b   c   d

54 DIFFICULTY ✪✪✪✪✪✪✪✪✪✪ 2 Minutes

Three of the four pieces can be fitted together to form a perfect square.
Which is the odd piece out?

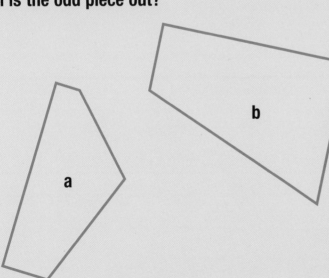

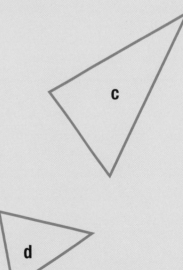

55 DIFFICULTY ✪✪✪✪✰✰✰✰✰✰  4 Minutes

Given that scales a and b balance perfectly, how many green balls are needed to balance scale c?

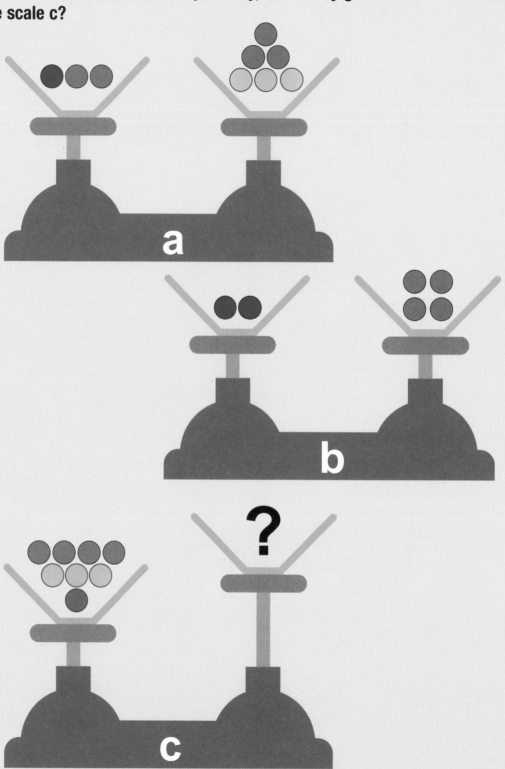

56 DIFFICULTY ✪✪✪✪✪✩✩✩✩✩  2 Minutes

Study this picture for two minutes, then see if you can answer the questions on page 48.

57 DIFFICULTY ✪✪✪✪✪✪✪✩✩✩ 3 Minutes

Which shape (a, b, or c) goes in the empty triangle?

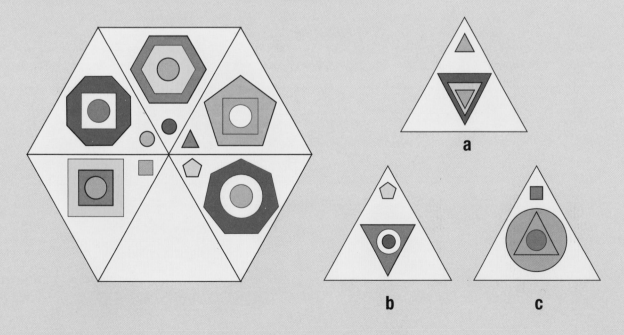

a

b

c

[56] DIFFICULTY ☆☆☆☆☆☆☆☆☆  2 Minutes

Can you answer these questions about the puzzle on page 47 without looking back?

1. What color is the fruit bowl?

2. Which fruit lies partially hidden behind the bowl?

3. How many limes are there in the bowl?

4. How many oranges are there in the bowl?

5. How many strawberries are there on the tray?

6. What is the total number of pieces of fruit in the bowl?

7. How many leaves are there on each apple: none, one, or two?

8. How many cherries are there on the tray?

58 DIFFICULTY ☆☆☆☆☆☆☆☆☆  3 Minutes

In pair c, where should the minute hand be pointing?

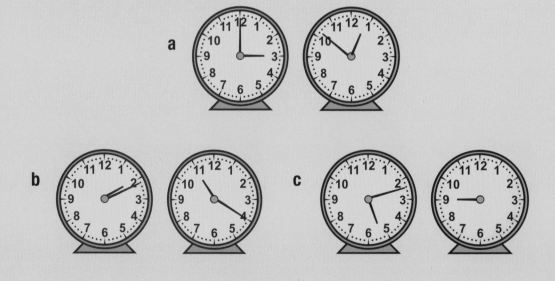

59 DIFFICULTY ✪✪✪✪✪✪✪☆☆☆  **5** Minutes

Can you fit the colored shapes below into the shaded area in this tangram puzzle? Pieces may be rotated, but not flipped over, and no piece may overlap another.

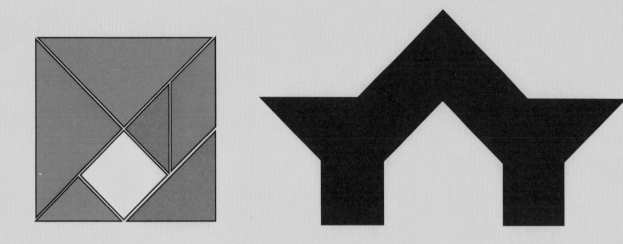

60 DIFFICULTY ✪✪✪✪✪✪✪☆☆☆  **5** Minutes

Again, can you fit the colored shapes below into the shaded area in this tangram puzzle? Pieces may be rotated, but not flipped over, and no piece may overlap another.

61 DIFFICULTY ✪✪✪✪✪✪✪✪✪  **5** Minutes

Which of the four boxed figures (a, b, c, or d) completes the set?

62 DIFFICULTY ✪✪✪✪✪✪✪✩✩✩

 **Minutes**

Can you spot the ten differences between these two pictures? Circle them in the bottom drawing.

63 DIFFICULTY ✪✪✪✪✪✩✩✩✩✩ ⏰ 4 Minutes

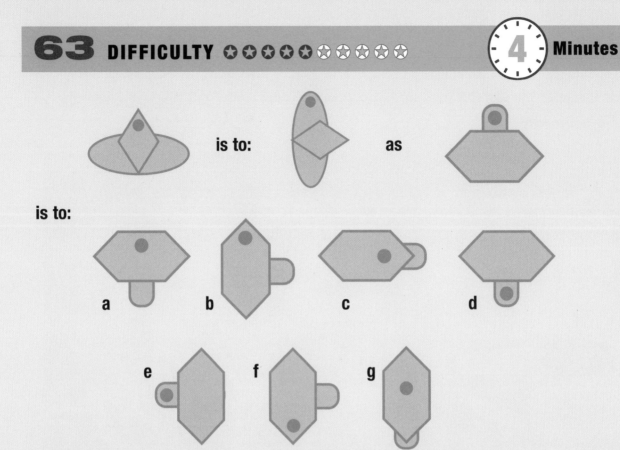

is to:

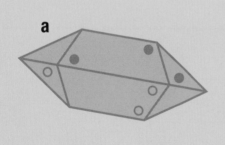

a   b   c   d

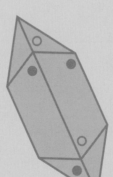

e   f   g

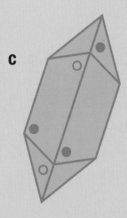

64 DIFFICULTY ✪✪✪✩✩✩✩✩✩✩ ⏰ 1 Minute

Which of these shapes is the odd one out?

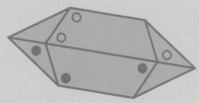

a   b   c

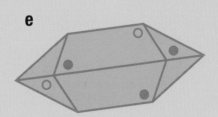

d   e

65 DIFFICULTY ✪✩✩✪✪✪✩✩✩✩    Minutes

In this game of solitaire, the aim is to jump one blue disk over another (horizontally or vertically), removing the disk you jumped over from the board until only one piece remains. Jumps can occur only over one disk and you must land on an empty space. The aim is to end up with just one blue disk remaining.

On this unusual board, a few of the squares are left blank. You must remain within the area marked out by the game board at all times. There may be more than one solution to the game. You could use a piece of squared paper and some coins to play this game.

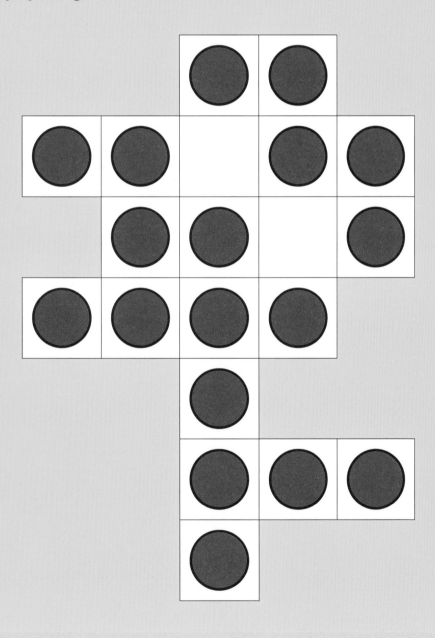

66 DIFFICULTY ✪✩✩✪✩✪✩✩✩✩  **4** Minutes

When the shape below is folded to form a cube, which of the following (a, b, c, d, or e) can be produced?

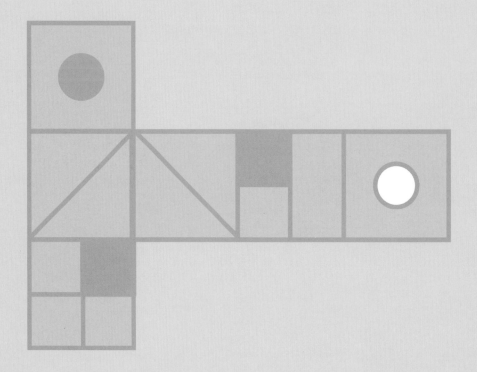

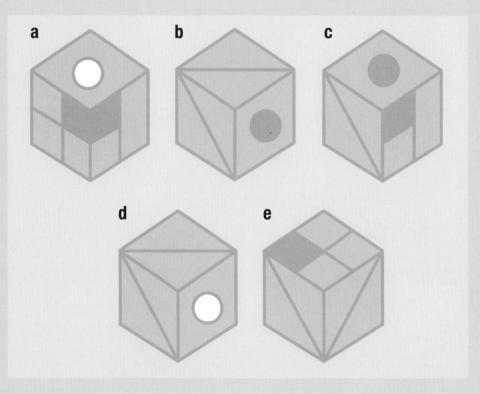

67 DIFFICULTY ✪✪✪✪✪✪✪☆☆☆  4 Minutes

Can you fit the colored shapes below into the shaded area in this tangram puzzle? Pieces may be rotated, but not flipped over, and no piece may overlap another.

68 DIFFICULTY ✪✪✪✪☆☆☆☆☆☆  3 Minutes

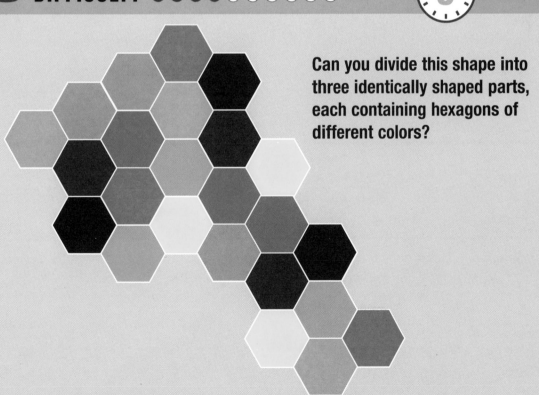

Can you divide this shape into three identically shaped parts, each containing hexagons of different colors?

69 DIFFICULTY ✪✪✪✪✪✪✪☆☆☆

5 Minutes

Can you fit the colored shapes below into the shaded area in this tangram puzzle? Pieces may be rotated, but not flipped over, and no piece may overlap another.

70 DIFFICULTY ✪✪✪✪✪✪☆☆☆☆

5 Minutes

Can you color this map using yellow, red, blue, and green only so that no two touching areas are the same? This rule doesn't apply to areas that touch at a corner point only.

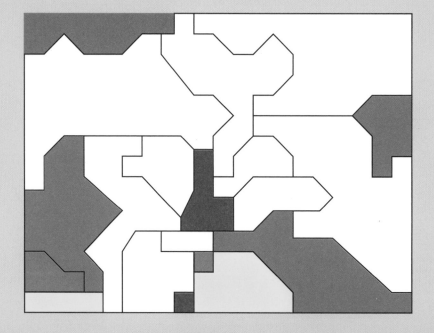

71 DIFFICULTY ✪✪✪✪✪✪✪✪✪✪  **Minutes**

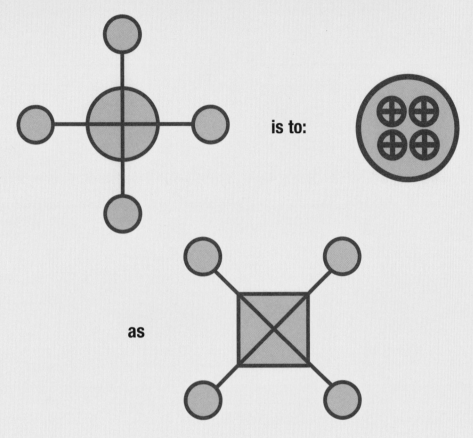

is to:

as

is to:

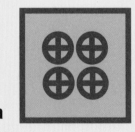

a

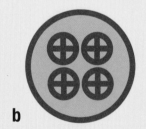

b

c

d

e

72 DIFFICULTY ⭐⭐⭐⭐⭐☆☆☆☆☆ **4** Minutes

Can you spot the eight differences between these two sets of hot air balloons? Circle the differences in the bottom set.

73 DIFFICULTY ✪✪✪✪✪✪✪☆☆☆  **Minutes**

Can you fit the colored shapes below into the shaded area in this tangram puzzle? Pieces may be rotated, but not flipped over, and no piece may overlap another.

74 DIFFICULTY ✪✪✪✪✪☆☆☆☆☆  **Minutes**

At 23:15 on Thursday, January 30, you were sailing west aboard a liner in the Pacific. Three and a half hours later you realized you had crossed the International Date Line, so you decided to write a letter. What day, month, and time did you write at the top?

75 DIFFICULTY ✪✪✪✪✪✪☆☆☆☆  5 Minutes

Can you color this map using yellow, red, blue, and green only so that no two touching areas are the same? This rule doesn't apply to areas that touch at a corner point only.

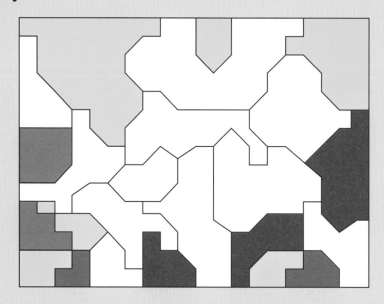

76 DIFFICULTY ✪✪✪✪✪✪☆☆☆☆  4 Minutes

Can you fit the colored shapes below into the shaded area in this tangram puzzle? Pieces may be rotated, but not flipped over, and no piece may overlap another.

77 DIFFICULTY ✪✪✪✪✪✩✩✩✩✩ ⏱ **3** Minutes

Which of the four boxed figures (a, b, c, or d) completes the set?

?

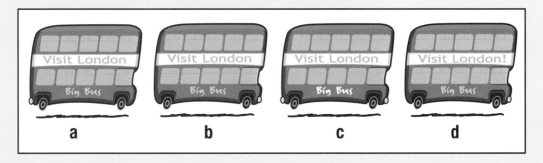

a   b   c   d

78 DIFFICULTY ★☆☆★☆☆☆☆☆☆  Minutes

Which of the four boxed figures (a, b, c, or d) completes the set?

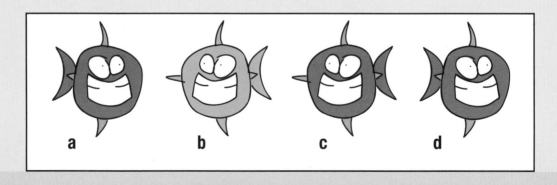

a   b   c   d

79 DIFFICULTY ✪✪✪✪✪✪✪✩✩✩  Minutes

Mr. Smith is away on business. His partner Mr. Jones needs access to the company safe. The only items on Mr. Smith's desk are these matchsticks. Can you help Mr. Jones crack the code to find the combination to the safe?

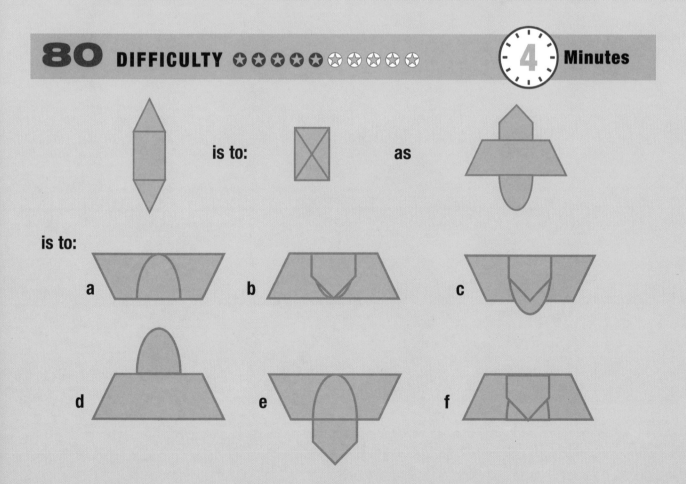

80 DIFFICULTY ✪✪✪✪✪✪✪✩✩✩ 4 Minutes

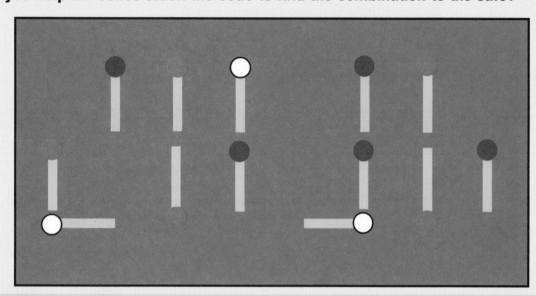

81 DIFFICULTY ✪✪✪✪✪✪✪✪✪✪ ⑤ Minutes

Can you fit the colored shapes below into the shaded area in this tangram puzzle? Pieces may be rotated, but not flipped over, and no piece may overlap another.

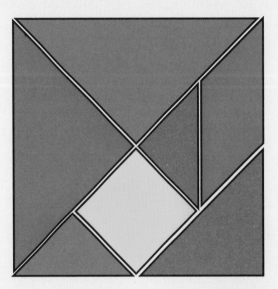

82 DIFFICULTY ★★★★★★☆☆☆☆ ⏱ 8 Minutes

In each of the four buildings below, one type of brick is used more or less frequently than it is in the other three buildings. Can you determine the different brick in each construction? The ten brick types are as follows:

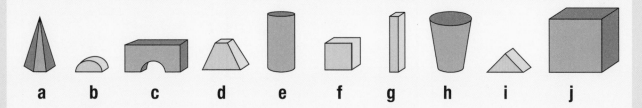

a   b   c   d   e   f   g   h   i   j

Building 1

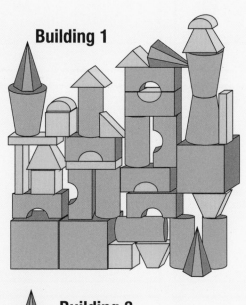

Building 2

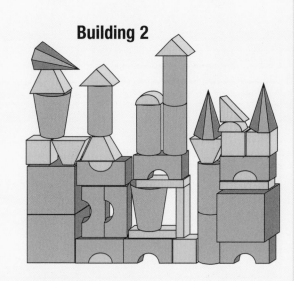

Building 3

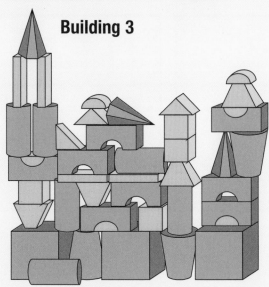

Building 4

83 DIFFICULTY ★☆★☆★☆☆★☆☆

Place the pictures in order so that the story makes narrative sense.

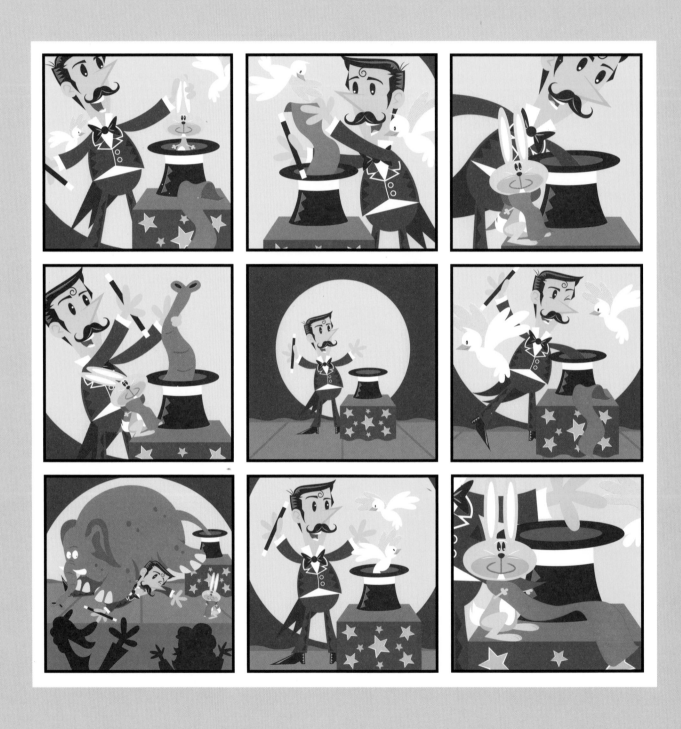

84 DIFFICULTY ✪✩✩✪✩✪✩✪✩✩✪  **4** **Minutes**

What time should be displayed on the fourth clock?

85 DIFFICULTY ⭐✩⭐✩✩✩✩✩✩✩  **Minutes**

Sara's magic mirror reflects very strangely! Can you match each vase to its correct (although misplaced and somewhat distorted) image in the mirror?

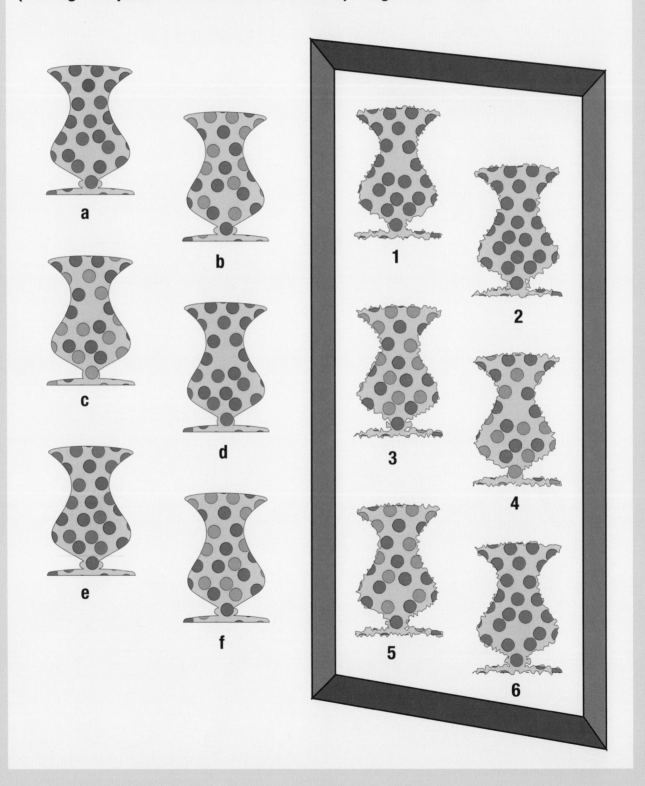

86 DIFFICULTY ✪✪✪✪✪✩✩✩✩✩  **Minutes**

Which five pieces can be fitted together to form an identical copy of this crown? Pieces may be rotated, but not flipped over.

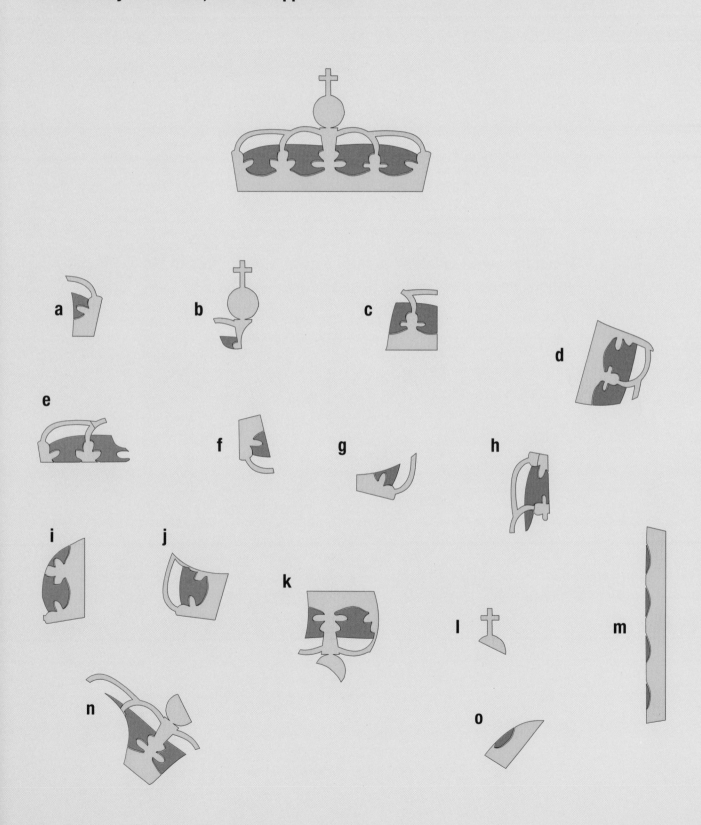

87

DIFFICULTY ✪✪✪✪✪✪✩✩✩✩

3 Minutes

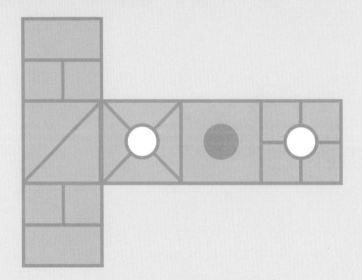

When the above is folded to form a cube, which three of the options below (a, b, c, d, or e) can be produced?

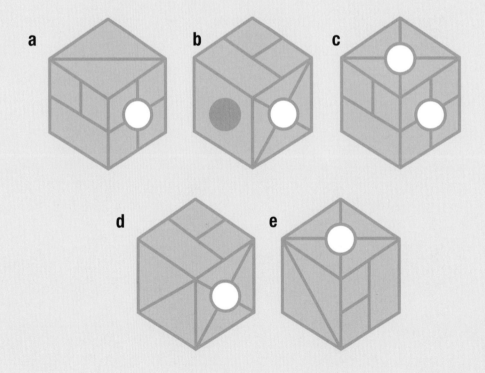

88 DIFFICULTY ✪✪✪✪✪✪✪✪✪✪

 **Minutes**

Two of these rugs are identical. Can you spot the pair?

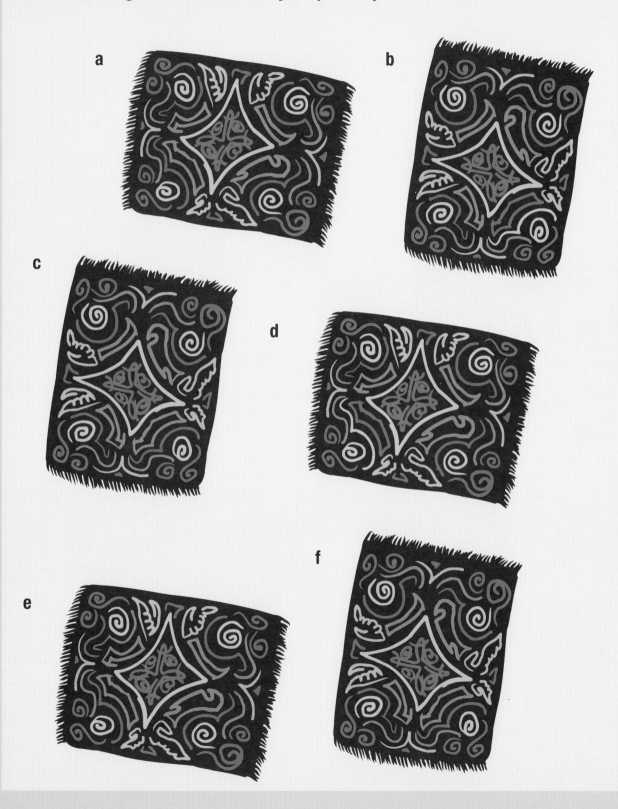

a

b

c

d

e

f

89

DIFFICULTY ✪✪✪✩✩✩✩✩✩✩  3 Minutes

There are eight differences between these two pictures. Can you spot them? Circle them in the lower drawing.

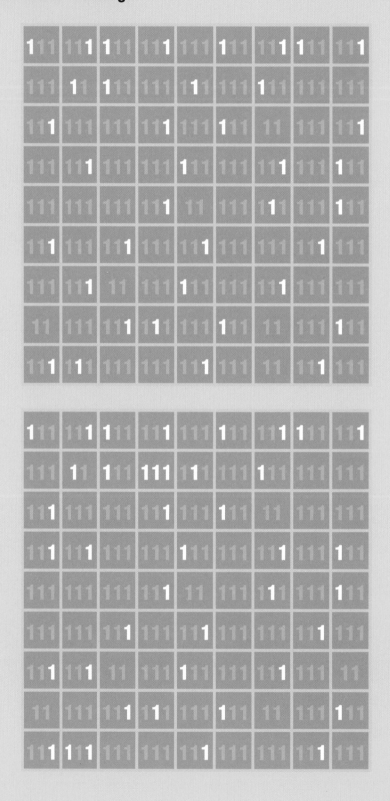

90 DIFFICULTY ⍟⍟⍟⍟⍟⍟⍟☆☆☆  **5** Minutes

Can you divide this grid into four sections, each containing stars of five different colors?

91 DIFFICULTY ⍟⍟⍟⍟⍟⍟☆☆☆☆ **3** Minutes

Can you fit the colored shapes into the shaded area in this tangram puzzle? Pieces may be rotated, but not flipped over, and no piece may overlap another.

92 DIFFICULTY ✪✪✪✪✪✪✪☆☆☆  Minutes

Find a way for the green caterpillar to reach his little pink friend without encountering a spider.

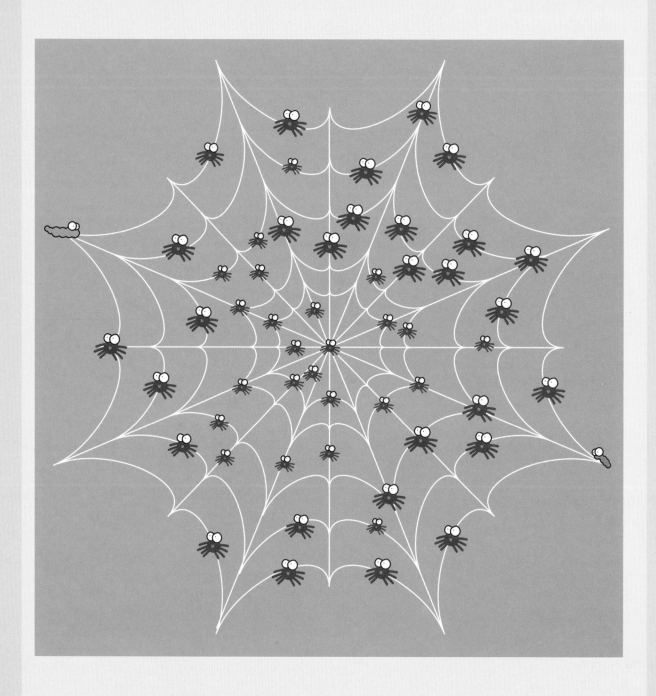

93 **DIFFICULTY** ✪✪✪✪✪✩✩✩✩✩  **Minutes**

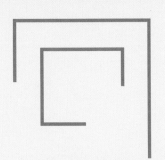

is to:

as

is to:

a **b**

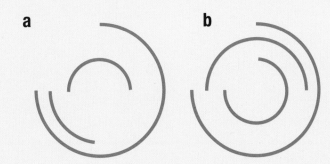

c **d** **e**

 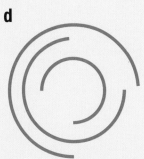 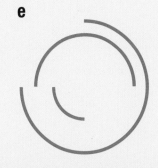

94 DIFFICULTY ✪✪✪✪☆☆☆☆☆☆  5 Minutes

Based on the hand positions of the other clocks, where should the minute hand of the first clock be pointing?

95 DIFFICULTY ✪✪✪✪✪✪✪☆☆☆ 3 Minutes

Without using a ruler, can you figure out how many straight lines are in this figure?

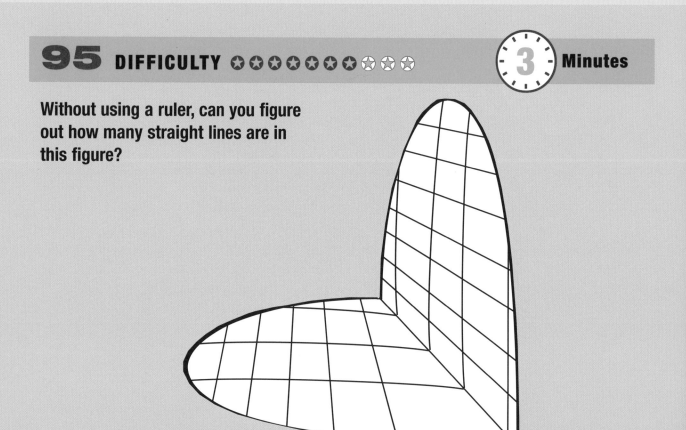

96 **DIFFICULTY** ✪✪✪✪✪✪✪✪✪✪  **Minutes**

In the pyramid of balls below, what color should the missing ball be?

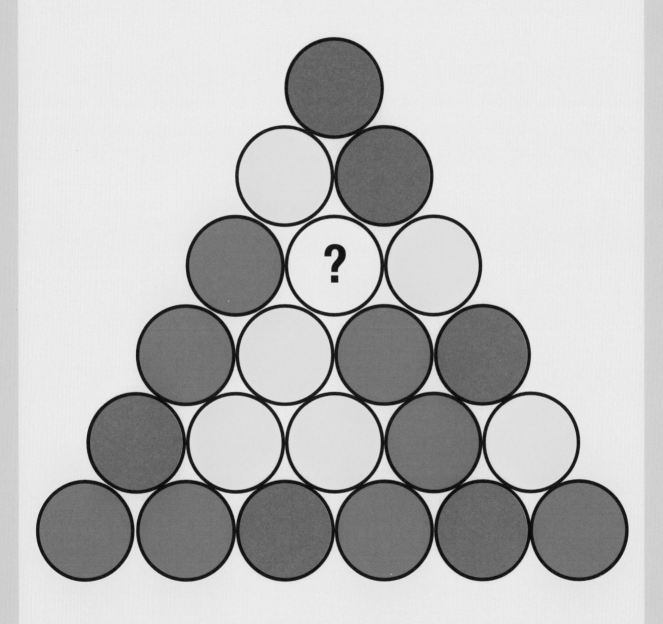

97 DIFFICULTY ✪✪✪✪✪✪✪✪✪✪

30 Minutes

Make the connections between the numbers to complete this numbergram. See page 20 for instructions on how to complete this kind of puzzle. Jump to it!

Column clues (top of grid):

						2																9								
				2	2	2															10	3								
				8	4	3	1	3													4	1	7							
			6	3	3	4	3	4	7																					
	5	5	2	1	1	1	6	7	9	18		12	12	13		18	18	18	17	2	2	7		16						
2	4	1	2	1	1	1	1	2	5	3	3	23	9	7	3	15	1	1	1	1	2	1	3	17	3	16	13	9	5

Row clues (left of grid):

			3
			7
		3	4
	4	1	4
	5	2	8
		6	11
			23
			24
		5	13
		2	15
			23
			23
			23
			22
		15	5
	5	8	7
	5	6	8
	5	5	8
	4	5	8
	4	5	7
	4	5	6
	4	5	6
	3	5	4
		4	4
		4	7
		8	7
3	1	1	1
1	1	1	1
1	1	1	1
	1	1	1

98 DIFFICULTY ✪✪✪☆☆☆☆☆☆☆  **Minutes**

Take three large coins and arrange them to make an equilateral triangle.

99 DIFFICULTY ✪✪✪✪✪☆☆☆☆☆  **Minutes**

In this sequence, what should the hour hand of clock d point to?

100 DIFFICULTY ★★★★★★★☆☆☆

5 Minutes

Can you put the pieces together to form a 10 x 10 square in which each row and column adds up to the same total?

17	79	42	89	50
78	54	63	84	36
96	18	30	92	73

1	95	52	59
	31	22	
	60	64	
	5	76	
	66	62	

	29
24	80	82
77	28	11
90	6	98
12	3	88

21	
56	67
9	2
85	44
53	94

87	35
37	47
81	71

45	13	65	68
32			70
97			10
51			26

14
61

86	49	20	100	25	15
19	7	91	33	57	23

93
74

43	83	39
55	38	27
16	58	99

72	75	4	48	40	69	34	41
46	8						

101 DIFFICULTY ✪✪✪✪✩✩✩✩✩✩

 **3** Minutes

Which of the four boxed figures (a, b, c, or d) completes the set?

102 DIFFICULTY ✪✪✪✪✪✪✪✩✩✩  6 Minutes

This white grid holds the twelve colored pieces in such a way that no piece comes into contact with another of the same color. Pieces may be rotated or flipped over. The black circles on the pieces should be aligned over the black circles in the grid. Can you determine how every piece should be placed?

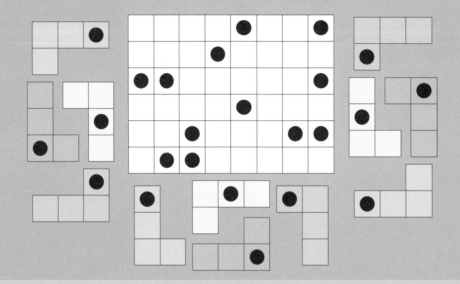

103 DIFFICULTY ✪✪✪✪✪✪✪✩✩✩  5 Minutes

Can you color this map using yellow, red, blue, and green only so that no two touching areas are the same? This rule doesn't apply to areas that touch at a corner point only.

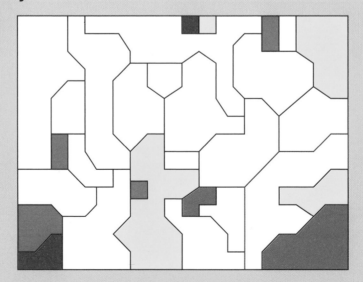

104 DIFFICULTY ✪✪✪✪✪✪✪✪✪✪  Minutes

Place the remaining cards to the left of the colored grid so that each horizontal row and vertical column contains a joker, ace, two, three, four, five, and six of hearts. Each shape (shown by the different colors) should also contain a joker, ace, two, three, four, five, and six of hearts. Some cards are already in their correct positions.

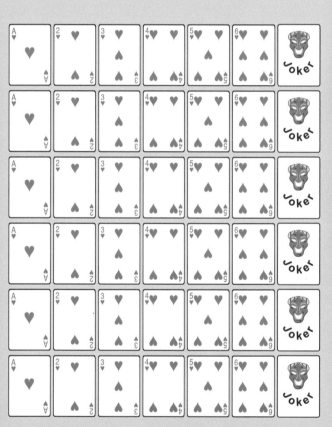

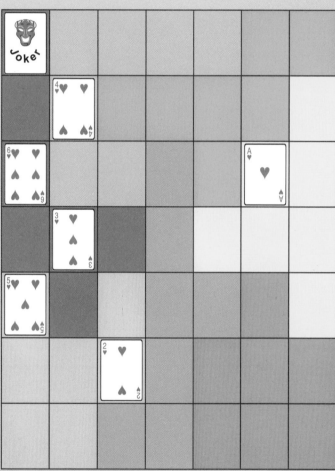

105 DIFFICULTY ✪✪✪✪✪✪☆☆☆☆

In the game of solitaire, the aim is to jump one blue disk over another (horizontally or vertically), removing the disk you jumped over from the board. Jumps can occur only over one disk, and you must land into an empty space. The aim is to end up with just one blue disk remaining.

On this unusual board, a few of the squares have been left blank (as indicated by the small circles or pegs). You must remain within the area marked out by the game board at all times. There may be more than one solution. You could use a piece of squared paper and some coins to play this game.

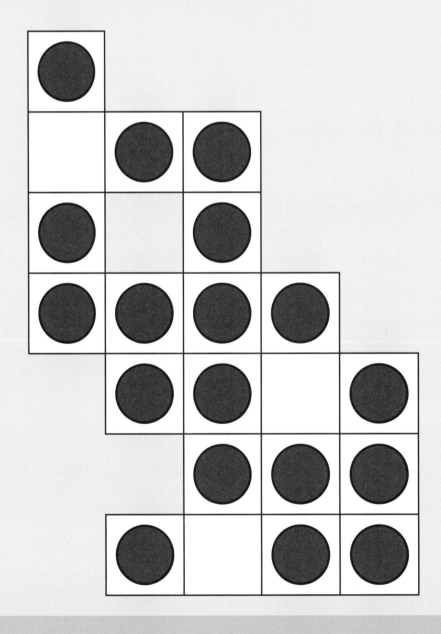

106 DIFFICULTY ✪✪✪✪✪✪✪✪✪✪  **2** Minutes

Study this picture for two minutes, then see if you can answer the questions on page 86.

107 DIFFICULTY ✪✪✪✪✪✪✪✪✪✪  **2** Minutes

Which of the following shapes is the odd one out?

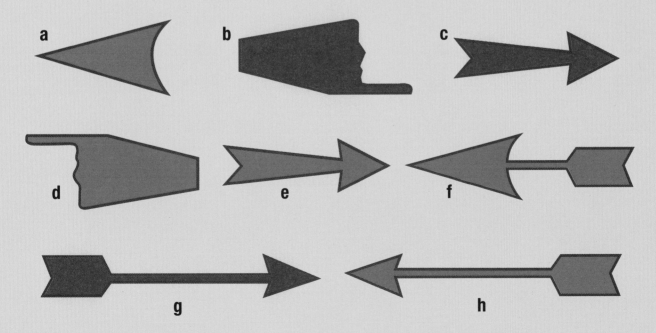

[106] DIFFICULTY ✪✪✪✪✪✪✩✩✩

Can you answer these questions about the puzzle on page 85 without looking back?

1. How many men are wearing green sweaters?

2. How many men have brown hair and no mustache?

3. Which letter identifies the only man wearing a brown sweater?

4. How many men have downturned mouths?

5. How many men with blond hair are wearing glasses?

6. How many men have mustaches of the same color as both their hair and their beards?

7. Which letters identify the two men with gray mustaches?

8. Which letters identify the men wearing red sweaters?

108 DIFFICULTY ✪✪✪✪✪✪✩✩✩✩  Minutes

Can you fit the colored shapes below into the shaded area in this tangram puzzle? Pieces may be rotated, but not flipped over, and no piece may overlap another.

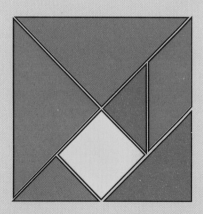

109 DIFFICULTY ✪✪✪✪✪✪✪✪✪  Minutes

Can you spot the nine differences between these two pictures?
Circle them in the lower drawing.

Which of the four boxed figures (a, b, c, or d) completes the set?

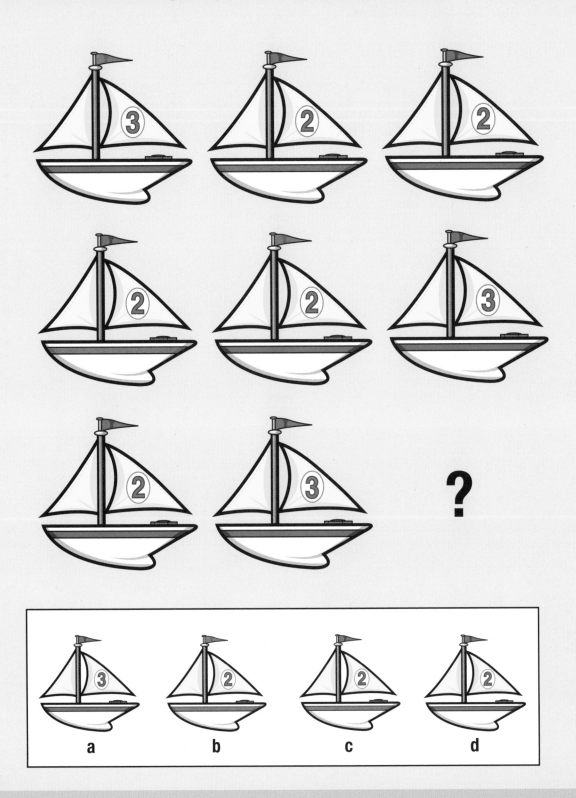

111 DIFFICULTY ✪✪✪✪✪✪✪☆☆☆

 Minutes

Keith's magic mirror reflects very strangely! Can you match each candle to its correct (although misplaced and somewhat distorted) image in the mirror?

112 DIFFICULTY ✪✪✪✪✪✪☆☆☆☆ ⏱ **3** Minutes

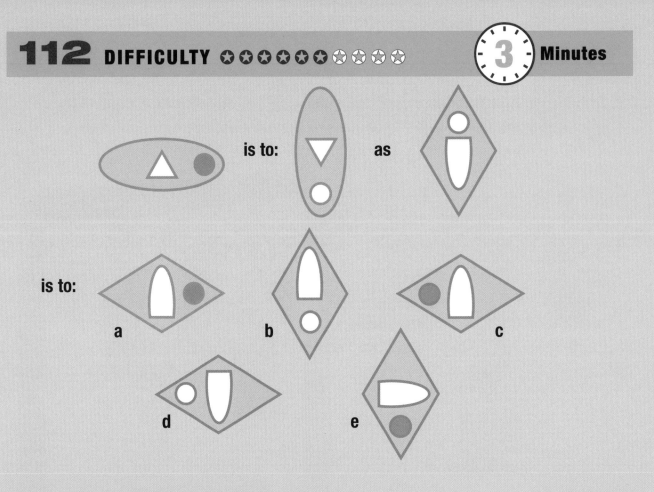

is to:

a   b   c

d   e

113 DIFFICULTY ✪✪✪✪✪✪☆☆☆☆ ⏱ **3** Minutes

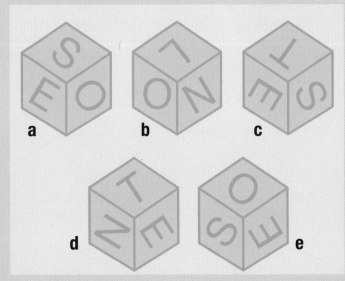

a   b   c

d   e

When the above is folded to form a cube, which of the options opposite (a, b, c, d, or e) is the only one that can't be produced?

114 DIFFICULTY ✪✪✪✪✪✪✪✩✩✩  3 Minutes

Can you fit the colored shapes below into the shaded area in this tangram puzzle? Pieces may be rotated, but not flipped over, and no piece may overlap another.

115 DIFFICULTY ✪✪✪✪✪✪✪✩✩✩  6 Minutes

Which five pieces fit together to match the envelope below? Pieces may be rotated, but not flipped over.

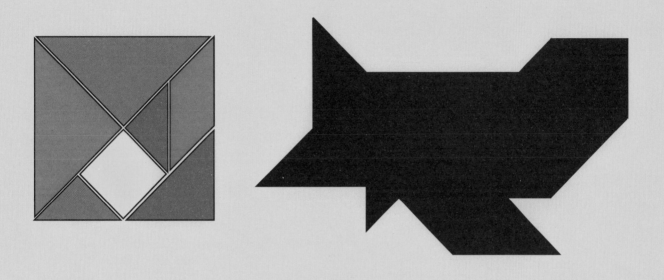

116 DIFFICULTY ✪✪✪✪✪✪✪✪✪✪

 **5** Minutes

Weigh up the symbols below. Given that scales a and b balance perfectly, how many hearts are needed to balance scale c?

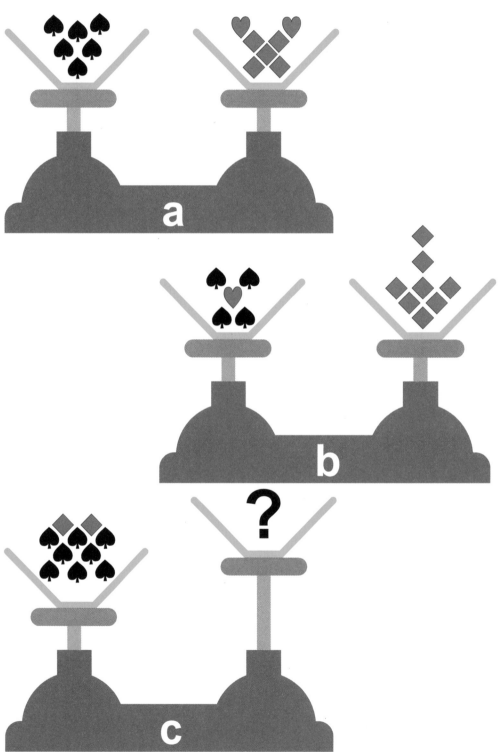

117 DIFFICULTY ✪✪✪✪✪✪✪✪✪✪  Minutes

**Can you spot the seven differences between these two pictures?
Circle them in the lower drawing.**

118 DIFFICULTY ✪✪✪✪✪✪✪✪✪✪  10 Minutes

Kirsty played a game of Snakes and Ladders with her brother Tom, who threw the first 6, so started first, placing his playing piece on the 6. After that, every time it was Kirsty's turn, her die followed the sequence 5, 4, 2, 6, 3, 1; so her first move was to square 5, then square 9, etc. After his first turn when he threw the 6, Tom's die followed the sequence 4, 5, 1, 3, 2, 6 each time, so his second move was to square 10, which took him up the ladder to square 30, and his third move was to square 35, etc. The normal rules of the game were followed, so whenever someone landed on a square that had the foot of a ladder, the piece was moved to the top of the ladder. Whenever someone landed on a square that had the head of a snake, the piece was moved to the tail of the snake. The number thrown to end the game didn't necessarily matter, since the first person to move a piece completely off the board won. Who won the game—Kirsty or Tom?

100	99	98	97	96	95	94	93	92	91
81	82	83	84	85	86	87	88	89	90
80	79	78	77	76	75	74	73	72	71
61	62	63	64	65	66	67	68	69	70
60	59	58	57	56	55	54	53	52	51
41	42	43	44	45	46	47	48	49	50
40	39	38	37	36	35	34	33	32	31
21	22	23	24	25	26	27	28	29	30
20	19	18	17	16	15	14	13	12	11
1	2	3	4	5	6	7	8	9	10

START →

119 DIFFICULTY ✪✪✪✪✪✪✪✪✪✪

3 Minutes

Can you find a way for the sheep to reach her lunch?

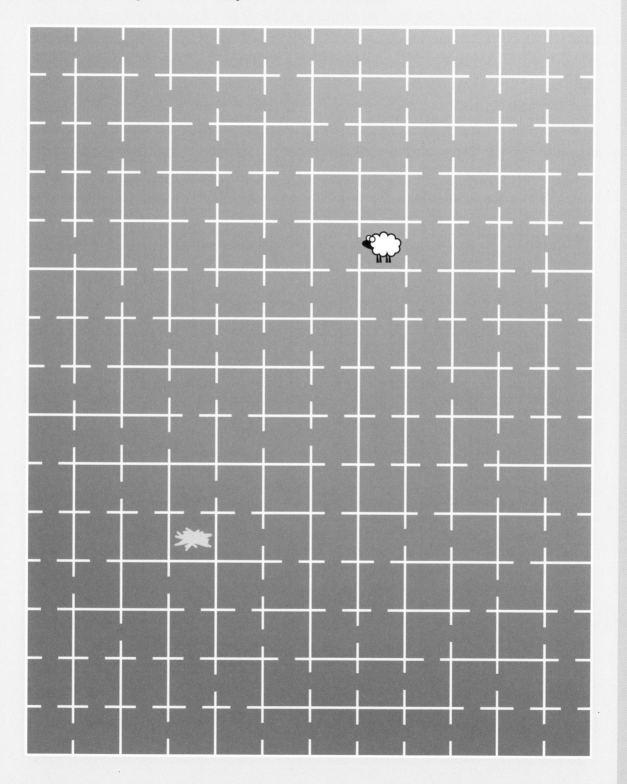

120 DIFFICULTY ✪✪✪✪✪✪✪✪✪✪  30 Minutes

Make the connections between the numbers to complete this numbergram. See page 20 for instructions on how to complete this kind of puzzle. Once you start, you'll soon be galloping along.

Top clues:

```
                        4  3  4
                        6  3  3  3
                  3  5  4  4  3  4  7  6  5
            4  6  2  3  7  8 10  5  1  3  2  6  5  4        9  9
0  2  6  4  2 10  9  9  8  6  3  1  3  6  6  7  7  8  6  1 18 19 20 20 20 21 20 20 19 18
```

Left clues:

```
            1
         1  2
         2  3
         3  3
         2  4
      3  3  1
         8  3
         7  5
         7  6
            8
         8 10
         9 11
        10 12
      4  4 12
      3  2 11
      9  1 10
      9  3 10
      8  4 10
      5  5 10
   2  2  6 10
      5  7 10
      6  8 10
      8  6 11
      9  3 10
   1  8  1  9
      3  6  9
      3  5  8
         8  7
         6  6
            5
```

121 DIFFICULTY ✪✪✪✪✩✩✩✩✩✩

5 Minutes

Jane's magic mirror reflects very strangely! Can you match each butterfly to its correct (although misplaced and somewhat distorted) image in the mirror?

122 DIFFICULTY ✪✪✪✪✪✪✪✪✪ ⑤ Minutes

Which pieces fit together
to form an exact copy of
this arched gateway?
Pieces may be rotated,
but not flipped over.

a b

c d e f g

h i j l m

k

n o p q r

s t u v

w

x y z

123 DIFFICULTY ✪✪✪✪✪✪✪✪✪☆☆  **5** Minutes

Arrange these eighteen coins into eight rows of five coins each.

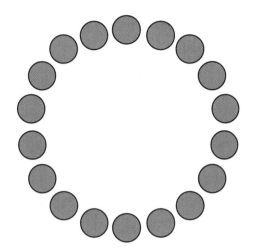

124 DIFFICULTY ✪✪✪✪✪✪☆☆☆☆ **2** Minutes

Can you fit the two sets of colored shapes below into the shaded area in this tangram puzzle? Pieces may be rotated, but not flipped over, and no piece may overlap another. (Hint: each figure is made up of one set of pieces.)

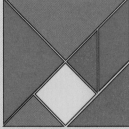

125 DIFFICULTY ✪✪✪✪✪✩✩✩✩✩  **5** Minutes

Which of the figures below (a, b, c, or d) completes the set?

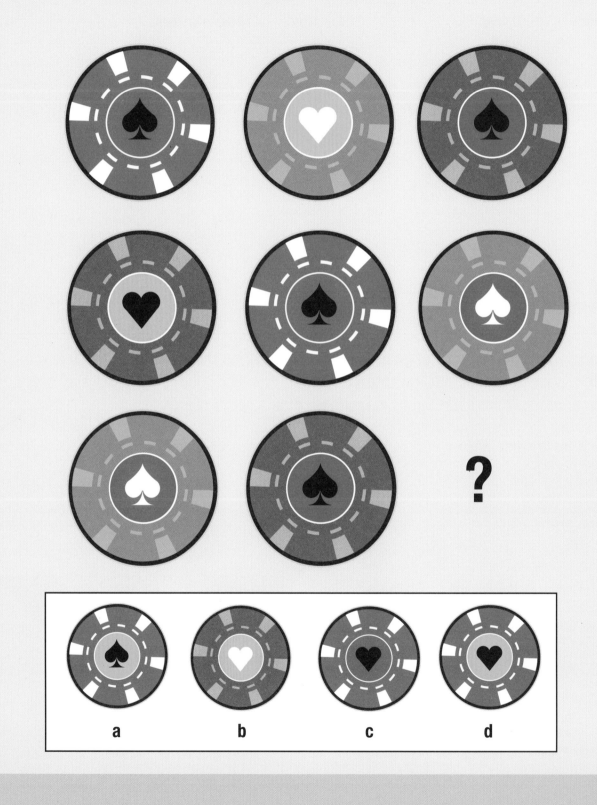

126 DIFFICULTY ✪✪✪✪✪✪✩✩✩✩

8 Minutes

In each of the four buildings below, one type of brick is used more or less frequently than it is in the other three buildings. Can you discover the different brick in each construction? The ten brick types are as follows:

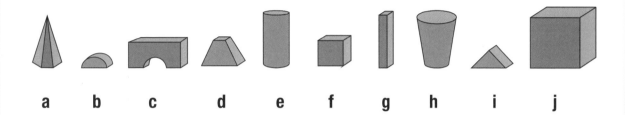

Building 1

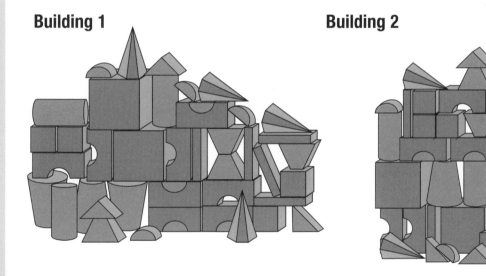

Building 2

Building 3

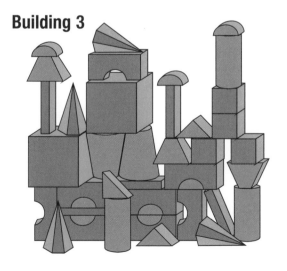

Building 4

127

DIFFICULTY ✪✪✪✪✪✪✪☆☆☆

Starting at the top row, move vertically and horizontally from any face on the top row to any face on the bottom row without moving diagonally, passing through any face that is winking, or moving from any face to another of the same color.

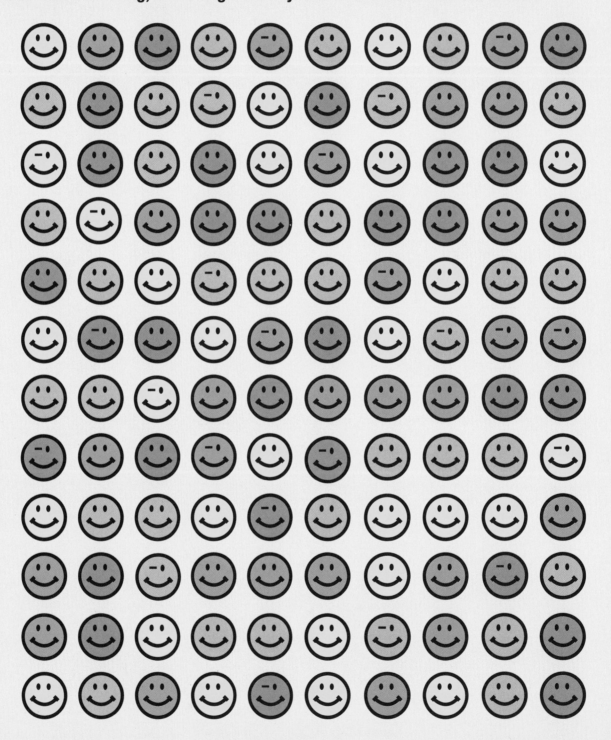

128 DIFFICULTY  4 Minutes

These dominoes have been placed in a spiral following a rule, but the first one placed has been turned over. Can you tell what it should be?

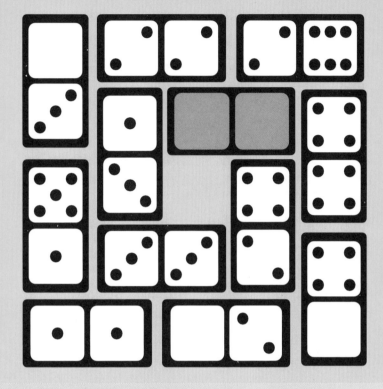

129 DIFFICULTY  2 Minutes

Study this picture for two minutes, then see if you can answer the questions on page 104.

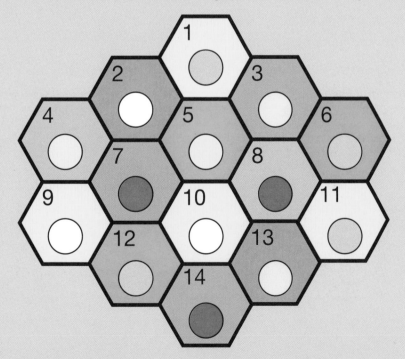

[129] DIFFICULTY ✪✪✪✪✪✪✪✪✪✪

Can you answer these questions about the puzzle on page 103 without looking back?

1. How many hexagons appear in the picture?

2. How many green hexagons appear?

3. How many red circles appear?

4. How many green hexagons contain red circles?

5. How many pink hexagons appear?

6. What is the total number of purple hexagons plus yellow hexagons?

7. What is the total number of pink hexagons containing blue circles plus yellow hexagons containing white circles?

8. What is the color of the circle in hexagon number 5?

130 DIFFICULTY ✪✪✪✪✪✪✪✪✪✪  5 Minutes

This white grid holds the twelve colored pieces surrounding it in such a way that no piece comes into contact with another of the same color. Pieces may be rotated or flipped over. The black circles on the pieces must align over the black circles in the grid. Can you determine how each piece should be placed?

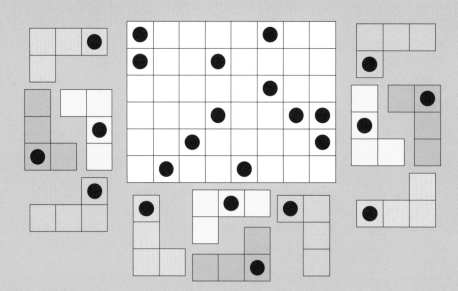

131 DIFFICULTY ✪✪✪✪✪✪✪✪✪✪  4 Minutes

What shape is missing from the center of the grid below?

ANSWERS

1

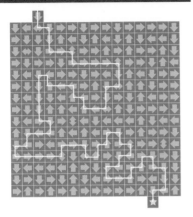

2

b; each is a square of paper with one fold.

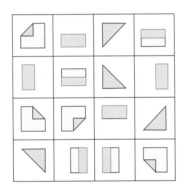

3

1. A
2. 3
3. red
4. H
5. Blue
6. Orange
7. Red
8. 14

4

5

6

Building 1   Building 2

a   i

Building 3   Building 4

b   e

7

d; each vertical and horizontal line contains two angels with a halo and one without. Each vertical and horizontal line contains one angel with a star on her headband and two without. Each vertical and horizontal line contains two angels with white shoes and one with pink shoes. Each vertical and horizontal line contains two angels with a pink headband and one with a white headband. Each vertical and horizontal line contains two angels with a heart in her hair and one without. Each vertical and horizontal line contains two angels with a white top and one with a pink top. The missing angel should have a halo, no star on her headband, pink shoes, a pink headband, a heart in her hair, and a white top.

8

a=3, b=5, c=1, d=2, e=6, and f=4

9

8; delete one triangle and one square from each side of scale a to give 1 circle = 2 triangles. Transpose this into scale b, thus 2 squares = 3 triangles. So 4 squares + 1 circle = 6 triangles + 2 triangles = 8 triangles. Thus 8 triangles are needed to balance scale c.

10

Kirsty won in the fewest moves.

11

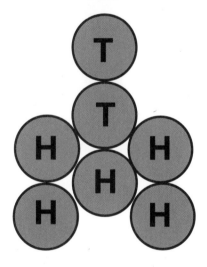

Push the central row of coins up to give two diagonal rows of heads.

12

c   e   j

13

14

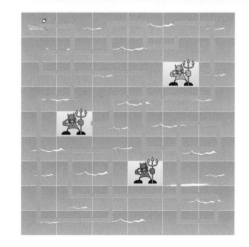

15

16

The tiles 5-1 and 5-2 have both been moved around 180 degrees.

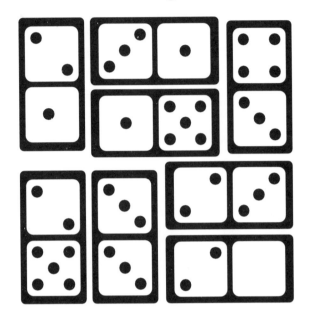

17

1=e, 2=d, 3=a, 4=f, 5=c, 6=b

18

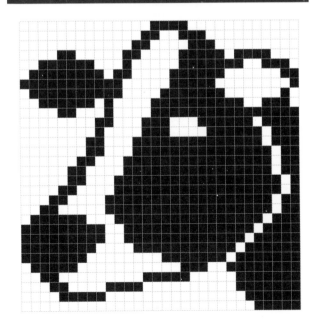

19

20

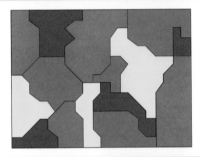

21

12; the number of minutes past the hour (shown by the minute hand) multiplied by the hour (shown by the hour hand) always equals 60: 30 x 2, 20 x 3, 10 x 6, 5 x 12.

22

d; the number of stars in each square of the middle row equals half the total of stars in the squares above and below.

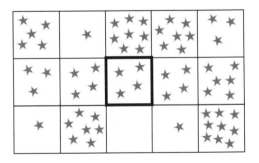

23

d; blue triangles turn to white circles and vice versa.

24

e

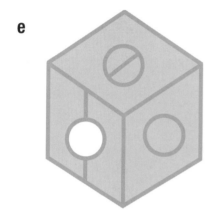

25

d; each vertical and horizontal line contains two mice with blue ears and one with white ears. Each vertical and horizontal line contains two mice with black noses and one mouse with a pink nose. Each vertical and horizontal line contains two mice with whiskers and one without. Each vertical and horizontal line contains one winking mouse and two mice that aren't winking. Each vertical and horizontal line contains two mice with tongues showing and one without. The missing mouse should have blue ears, a black nose, and whiskers. He should be winking and his tongue should be showing.

26

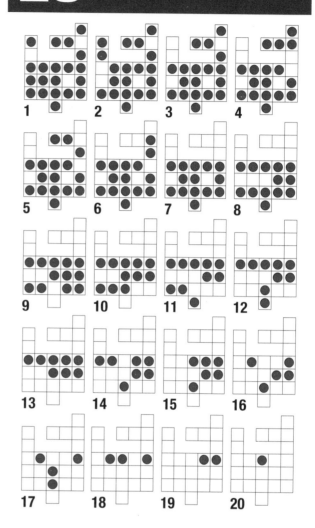

27

17:11, March 4, 2000.

28

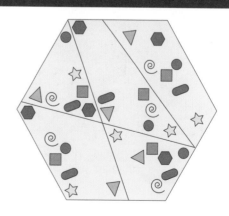

29

b and i
e and g

30

a and e

31

d; top moves to bottom, second moves to top, third moves to second, bottom moves to third.

32

The two squares second from the top left corner (marked with the arrows).

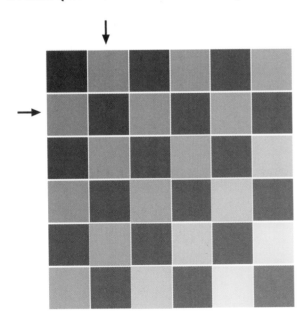

33

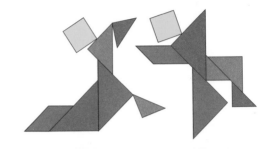

34

c

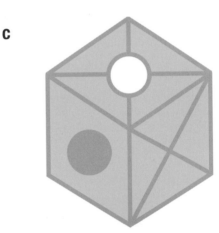

35

d; each vertical and horizontal line contains one drummer with a blue drum and two with red drums. Each vertical and horizontal line contains a drum with gold cord and two with white cord. Each vertical and horizontal line contains one yellow feather and two red ones. Each vertical and horizontal line contains one black mustache and two brown ones. Each vertical and horizontal line contains two black drum straps and one gold one. Each vertical and horizontal line contains two pairs of blue shoes and one brown pair. Each vertical and

horizontal line contains a blue, a white, and a red pair of drumsticks. The missing image should be of a drummer with a red drum with white cord. He should have a yellow feather, a brown mustache, gold drum straps, blue shoes, and blue drumsticks.

36

a; each vertical and horizontal line contains one background circle in green and two in pink. Each vertical and horizontal line  contains two pictures where the houses have chimneys and one where they don't. Each vertical and horizontal line contains one picture where the house windows are white and two where they are blue. Each vertical and horizontal line contains one picture where the house doors are white and two where they are blue. Each vertical and horizontal line contains one picture where there are four doors and two where there are only three. Each vertical and horizontal line contains one satellite dish pointing left, one pointing right, and one with no dish. The missing picture should have a green background circle, chimneys on the houses, blue windows, three blue doors, and no satellite dish.

37

Nine years. Each domino expresses a fraction; when added together, the total is nine.

38

7 objects are missing.

39

d; the white dot is in the square and triangle. In all the others it is in the circle and triangle.

40

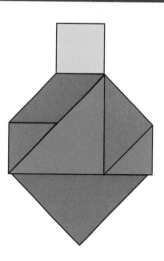

41

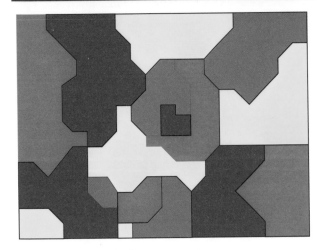

42

9; if you drew a line from the number 4 to the number 10 across the clock face, then clocks a and c would be mirror images of each other, so b and d must do likewise.

43

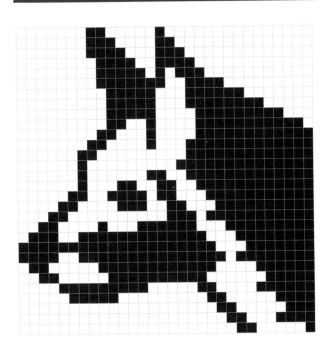

44

c; there are always as many black spots as there are vertical lines in each box.

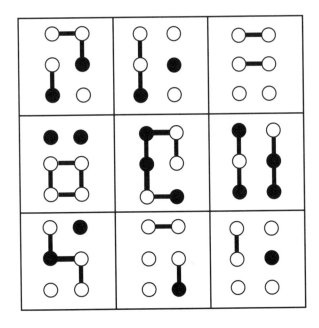

45

d

46

47

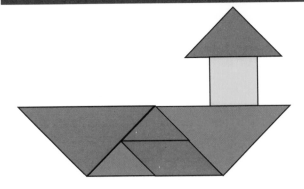

48

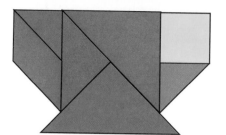

49

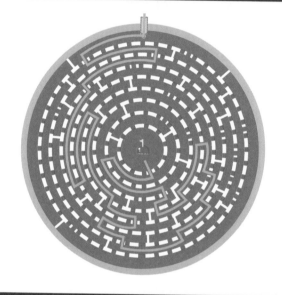

50

d and e

51

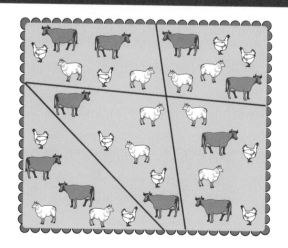

52

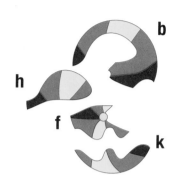

53

d; one is a mirror image of the other.

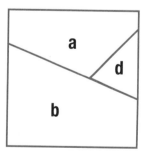

54

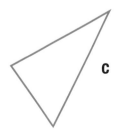

55

3; add one blue ball to both sides of scale a to give 1 green ball + 3 blue balls = 3 yellow balls + 4 blue balls, so 1 green ball = 3 yellow balls + 1 blue ball. From scale b, 1 green ball = 2 blue balls. Use this in the revised scale a, thus 2 blue balls = 3 yellow balls + 1 blue ball, so 1 blue ball = 3 yellow balls. Therefore scale c becomes 6 blue balls = 3 green balls. Thus, 3 green balls are needed to balance scale c.

56

1. Blue
2. Banana
3. 3
4. 2
5. 9
6. 8
7. 1
8. 10

57

a; all the triangles contain a total of 4 shapes and 12 corners.

58

10; on a 24-hour clock, each of the pair is the reverse of the other:
a = 15:00/00:51, b = 02:11/11:20, and c = 05:12/21:50. (On a digital clock, each number is also the other number upside down.)

59

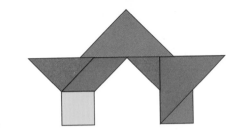

60

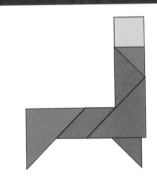

61

c; each vertical and horizontal line contains a car with a gold bumper and two with silver bumpers. Each vertical and horizontal line contains a car with a red gas cap and two with green gas caps. Each vertical and horizontal line contains two cars facing left and one facing right. Each vertical and horizontal line contains two cars with two wing mirrors and one with one wing mirror. Each vertical and horizontal line contains two cars with a rear bumper and one without a rear bumper. The missing picture should be of a car with a silver bumper and a red gas cap, facing left, with two wing mirrors and a rear bumper.

62

63

b; everything
rotates 90 degrees
clockwise, and the
dot transfers to
the top of the
other figure.

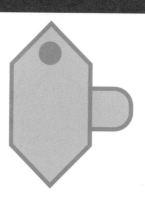

64

e; a is the same
figure as d
rotated and b is
the same figure
as c.

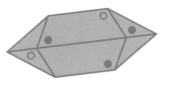

65

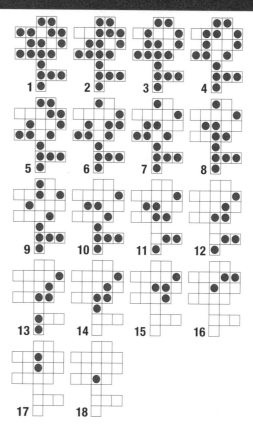

66

c

67

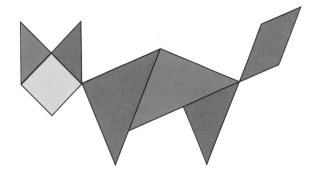

68

69

70

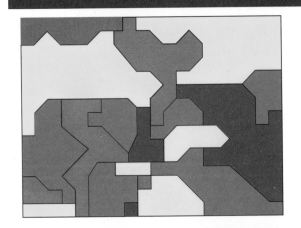

71

c; the cross transfers
to each of the circles
and the circles then
go inside the square.

72

73

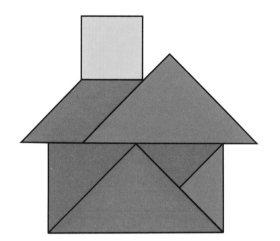

76

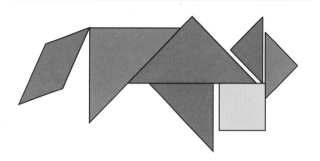

74

2:45 a.m. on Saturday, February 1: Traveling west over the IDL takes a traveler forward 24 hours, plus the 3 and a half hours of sailing.

77

b; each vertical and horizontal line contains two front bumpers, and two back bumpers in total. Each vertical and

horizontal line contains one bus with the words "Big Bus" in blue and two with white words. Each vertical and horizontal line contains a yellow, a green, and a white banner. Each vertical and horizontal line contains the words "Visit London" in white, pink, or black. Each vertical and horizontal line contains two buses with an exclamation mark at the end of "Visit London" and one without. The missing image should be of a bus with the back bumper missing, the words "Big Bus" in blue, and a white banner with the words "Visit London" in pink, without an exclamation mark.

75

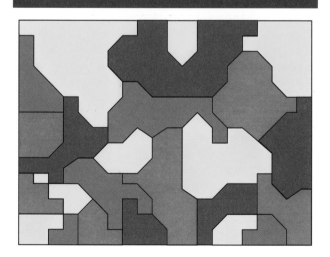

78

d; each vertical and horizontal line contains a blue fish, a green fish, and a red fish. Each vertical and horizontal line contains two fish with four fins and one fish with three fins. Each vertical and horizontal line contains two fish facing right and one facing left. The missing picture should be of a red fish, with four fins, facing right.

79

2836; for blue match heads, add a line to the left; for red match heads, add a line to the right; for white match heads, don't add a line.

80

f; the figures at the top and bottom fold into the middle figure.

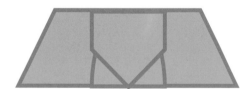

81

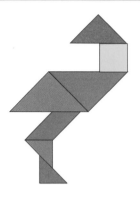

82

Building 1

f

Building 2

h

Building 3

b

Building 4

c

83

84

3:23; the hour hand value = number of sides x 3, and the minute hand value = the number of sides x 5. Triangle clock = 9:15. Rhomboid clock = 12:20. Hexagon clock = 18:30. Pentagon clock = 15:25.

85

a=6, b=5, c=4, d=1, e=2, and f=3

86

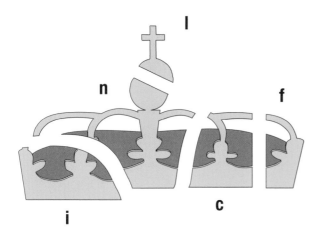

87

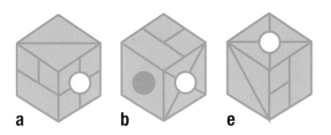

a   b   e

88

b and d

89

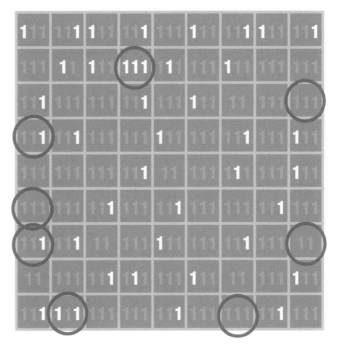

90

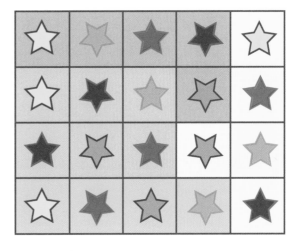

91

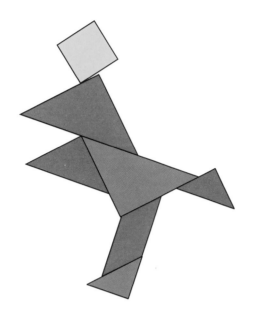

92

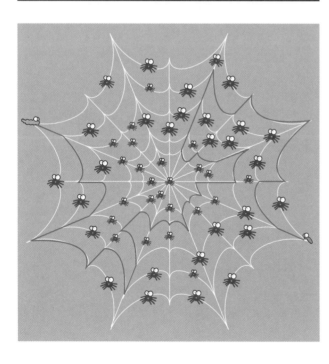

93

e; the two halves added together will produce three complete circles (two complete squares would be formed in the example).

94

The minute hand should point at the 5 to show 5:25. The minute is the square of the hour: 4:16, 6:36, 3:09, and 5:25.

95

15, which are shown in red. With the exception of the two that appear nearest, all the lines that run from side to side or up and down are slightly curved.

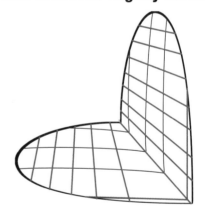

96

Blue; each triangle of six touching balls has three of one color, two of another, and one of the third color.

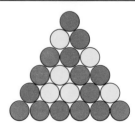

97

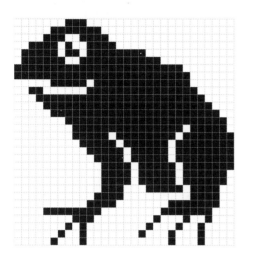

101

a; each vertical and horizontal line contains a pig with a blue nose, a pig with a white nose, and a pig with a pink nose. Each vertical and horizontal line contains a pig with a gold nose ring, a pig with a silver nose ring, and a pig with no nose ring. The missing picture should be of a pig with a white nose and a silver nose ring.

98

Place them on their edges, all touching. An equilateral triangle is formed in the middle.

102

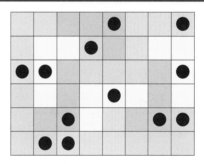

99

1; the minute hand value is always five times the hour hand value: 8:40, 4:20, 2:10, and 1:05.

103

100

104

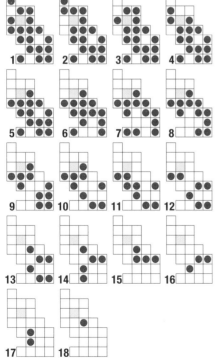

105

106

1. 2
2. None; every man in the picture has a mustache
3. g
4. 4
5. 2
6. 2
7. b and g
8. a, h, and l

107

e; in all the others, blue pointers are facing right and red pointers are facing left.

108

109

110

b; each vertical and horizontal line contains a number 3 boat and two number 2 boats. Each vertical and horizontal line contains two boats with a red flag and one with a blue flag. Each vertical and horizontal line contains two boats with a red stripe and one with a blue stripe. The missing picture should be of a number 2 boat with a blue flag and a blue stripe.

111

a=5, b=1, c=7, d=2, e=4, f=6, and g=3

112

a; the diamond and dot rotate 90 degrees clockwise, the dot changes from white to green (or vice versa), and the figure in the middle rotates 180 degrees.

113

d

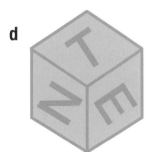

114

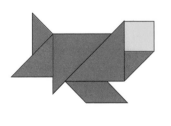

115

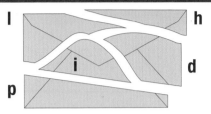

116

7; multiply scale a by 2, thus 10 diamonds + 4 hearts = 12 spades. Multiply scale b by 3, thus 3 hearts + 12 spades = 24 diamonds. Now replace the 12 spades in the revised scale b with their equivalent from the revised scale a, i.e., 10 diamonds + 4 hearts, so that now in scale b there are 3 hearts + 10 diamonds + 4 hearts = 24 diamonds, so 7 hearts = 14 diamonds, thus 1 heart = 2 diamonds. Apply this to the original scale a, i.e., replace the 2 hearts with 4 diamonds, so that 9 diamonds = 6 spades: thus 3 diamonds = 2 spades. Multiply scale a by 3, thus 15 diamonds + 6 hearts = 18 spades. Replace 15 diamonds with their value in spades (i.e., 10), so that 10 spades + 6 hearts = 18 spades, thus 6 hearts = 8 spades. In scale c, 2 diamonds = 1 heart and 8 spades = 6 hearts, thus 7 hearts are needed to balance scale c.

117

118

Tom wins in the fewest moves.

119

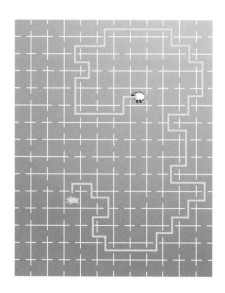

120

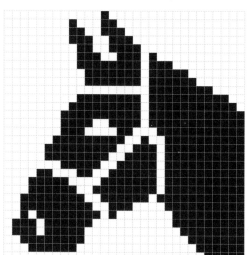

121

a=2, b=5, c=6, d=1, e=7, f=3, and g=4

122

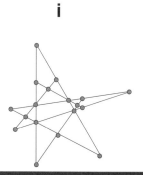

m j

w

a l

p

v b

g

e

i

123

124

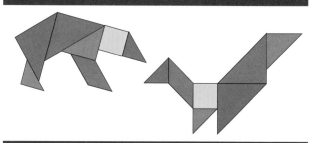

125

d; each vertical and horizontal line contains a red poker chip, a purple poker chip, and a green poker chip. Each vertical and horizontal line contains two red inner circles and one yellow inner circle. Each vertical and horizontal line contains one white symbol and two black symbols. Each vertical and horizontal line contains one heart and two spades. The missing picture should be of a red poker chip with a yellow inner circle and a black heart symbol.

126

Building 1
d

Building 2
e

Building 3
h

Building 4
g

127

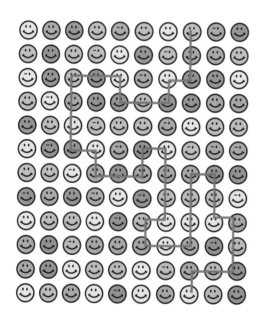

128

3-5. Each tile is followed by one bearing half its combined number of spots on the adjacent square (as in a game of dominoes). For example: 3-5 has a combined total of 8

spots, so must be followed by a domino bearing 4 spots on the adjacent square of the tile. (Note that the missing tile cannot be 4-4 because that has already been used.)

129

1. 14
2. 3
3. 3
4. 2
5. 3
6. 6
7. 4
8. Yellow

130

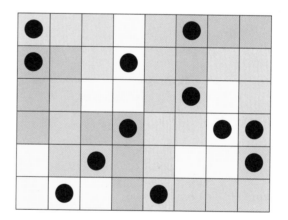

131

A square. Each edge between two grid squares has one shape corner touching it (outside edges don't count).

ACKNOWLEDGMENTS ✪ MIND'S EYE

✪ Puzzle contributors

Contributors are listed next to the numbers of the puzzles they created.

✪ David Bodycombe

Puzzles 20, 26, 41, 65, 70, 75, 102, 103, 105, 130

✪ Brainwarp

Puzzles 2, 4, 11, 16, 22, 32, 44, 46, 57, 95, 96, 98, 123, 128, 131

✪ Guy Campbell

Puzzles 1, 7, 15, 18, 25, 35, 36, 43, 49, 61, 77, 78, 83, 92, 97, 101, 110, 119, 120, 125, 127,

✪ Philip Carter

Puzzles 23, 24, 31, 34, 39, 45, 53, 54, 63, 64, 66, 71, 80, 87, 93, 107, 112, 113

✪ Filipa de Chassey

Puzzles 62 and 109

✪ Edward Phantera

Puzzles 29, 30, 50, 72, 88, 89, 100, 117

✪ Puzzle Press Ltd

Puzzles 3, 5, 6, 8, 9, 10, 12, 13, 14, 17, 19, 28, 51, 52, 55, 56, 68, 82, 85, 86, 90, 104, 106, 111, 115, 116, 118, 121, 122, 126, 129

✪ Justin Scroggie

Puzzles 21, 27, 37, 42, 58, 74, 79, 84, 94, 99

✪ Sunrise Puzzles

Puzzles 33, 40, 47, 48, 59, 60, 67, 69, 73, 76, 81, 91, 108, 114, 124

Mind's Eye was commissioned, edited, designed, and produced by:

Book Creation Ltd., 20 Lochaline Street, London W6 9SH, United Kingdom

Managing Director: Hal Robinson

Editor: David Popey   **Art Editor:** Keith Miller

Designer: Mark Sayer   **Copy Editors:** Sarah Barlow and Ali Moore